Praises for

Strangely Dim

Because the light of God's goodness is sometimes overshadowed by the dim realities of broken dreams and private anguish, Heather Anderson has written a deeply personal guide with the singular goal of helping us find our way again. She writes, not as a spectator from the stands, but as an active participant on the field of adversity. Her biblical insights will instruct you even as the story of her family inspires you. Read this book to be better prepared for the darkest days of your life.

—**Adam B. Dooley**, senior pastor, Englewood Baptist Church, Jackson, Tennessee, and author of *Hope When Life Unravels*

Not only did I enjoy the love story between Heather and Josh Anderson, but I also was drawn to the life lessons she has drawn from their lives. I appreciated Heather's transparency as well as the reminder that being separated from our dreams does not mean we are separated from God.

—**Mike Yorkey**, co-author of *Out of the Wilderness* and *At First Light*

We've all experienced situations where we don't understand God's plan. In these seasons we can choose to turn away from God and His purposes or turn to God and trust His providence. Heather sheds light into these inevitable dark times. Through this book, she guides us to a brighter future no matter how ***Strangely Dim*** our life may seem now.

—**Rachael Adams**, author of *A Little Goes a Long Way* and host of *The Love Offering* podcast

Heather thank you so much for taking us along this incredible journey with you. Many will be inspired to understand that God is with us through the ups and downs of life and that He always has a good plan for us. I pray this Holy Spirit inspired book will touch many lives for His glory!

—**Greg Gover**, SEKY-Fellowship of Christian Athletes Area Director

When we believe God is leading us in the direction of our dreams coming true or we experience what it feels like to live them for a while, it's devastating when our joy seems to be ripped from us without cause. In ***Strangely Dim***, Heather shares her family's story and walks us along the path of believing that God is good and can be trusted with our lives even when we can't see clearly. What a beautiful read!

—**Amanda Bacon**, co-author of *Shiny Things: Mothering on Purpose in a World of Distractions,* host of *At Night* podcast and co-host of *All the Mom Things* podcast

STRANGELY DIM

Discovering God's Light When Your Commitment to Him Leaves You in the Dark

---

Heather Anderson

Published by KHARIS PUBLISHING, imprint of KHARIS MEDIA LLC.

ISBN-13: 978-1-63746-128-0

ISBN-10: 1-63746-128-3

Library of Congress Control Number: 2022937363

All KHARIS PUBLISHING products are available at special quantity discounts for bulk purchase for sales promotions, premiums, fund-raising, and educational needs. For details, contact:

Kharis Media LLC
Tel: 1-479-599-8657
support@kharispublishing.com
www.kharispublishing.com

Contents

Introduction

Sitting on the edge of the couch, I watched him walk past me to the coffee pot. With my Bible laid open beside me, it wasn't long before he asked what I had been reading. The sun was beaming through the living room window onto my face, which made hiding my emotions even easier. As much as I looked forward to sharing my time with the Lord, I fought to hold back the sadness. Hot tears began running down my face as I glanced in his direction, and the only two words that I managed to utter were, "I'm sorry." I then turned towards our bedroom where our children were sleeping and told him I was sorry that our son would never watch him play.

After a few moments of silence, Josh understood that God confirmed to me what he already knew: his dream was over. He would never again make a diving catch, hear the crack of his bat, or beat out a ground ball. He would never again experience his heart racing as he dove on the ground to steal a base. He was now a former player.

Dreams don't last forever, but they sure are good while they last. Baseball was Josh's dream, and he worked his entire life to become a professional baseball player. Growing up in Eubank, Kentucky, becoming a Major League Baseball player was highly unlikely. No one from his hometown had ever accomplished such a feat. But God gave Josh a natural gift that others noticed from the time he was young. He was committed to the game, and he was committed to the Lord. Together they walked through valleys and stood on mountain peaks. At the height of his dream, however, God called him away. That's what brought us home.

Homes are places that meet us with comfort, familiarity, and rest. We know where everything is, and we know how each chair sits. The blankets are warm, and the couches are cozy. This is how my home feels. No matter how tough my day is, I know that I'll get to return to the security of that space. My relationship with God is like this. Growing up as a Christian from a very early age, I became very familiar with His ways, love, and shelter. But my husband losing his dream jeopardized that all-too-familiar space.

I say *his* dream, but in all reality, it became mine too. Becoming *one* takes on different meanings when you're married, because it's possible for your spouse's hobbies, interests, or pursuits to also become yours. This is especially true when you can't personally identify with a dream of your own. So, when your spouse dreams, you dream. When your spouse hurts, you hurt, because sometimes you can't provide the healing that's needed no matter what you do. But healing is what's needed. There are times we need healing from the *right* choices we've made.

When we love the Lord deeply, we often agree to His plans before realizing the weight of our decision. Our commitment to Him crushes our spirit, because we never anticipated waves of grief to knock us down over and over again. We then find ourselves surrounded by darkness without answers, explanations, or understanding. We want to deny our pain, believing that God will restore that which was taken. We may even question His actions, arguing that the best of who we are will never be again.

What's most damaging is cleaning up the aftermath of our loss. Dreams don't leave without sweeping through the depths of our hearts taking with them our confidence, security, and joy. Before we realize it, we've begun to withdraw from other pursuits, relationships, and endeavors. Life becomes meaningless as we drag ourselves to church, stare at our unopened Bibles, and watch as our prayers disappear between doubtful thoughts. Truly, our relationship with the Lord is what suffers most. It's not that we don't want to do His will; we are devastated that His plans don't include our dreams.

Pursuing a dream is no easy feat, because it requires dedication, hard work, and sacrifice. Many dreams are also time-sensitive, offering short windows for us to see them manifest in reality. Professional athletes, for example, usually do not play baseball, basketball, or football past their mid-40's. Not that surpassing this age makes the transition more manageable but changing careers after this point is more acceptable. There are fewer *why?* questions and more *what now?* "Why" questions are the most crushing, because we don't always have the answers. Can we say that we are retiring at the age of 28? Can we explain that our careers end because of injury when there are no signs of physical struggle? Can we claim that we're switching gears when there aren't any prospects in sight? That's darkness. When we can't provide answers to others and ourselves, it's difficult to see the path God has prepared for us.

Acceptance of our circumstances numbs the pain we are unable to explain. We tell ourselves that everything happens for a reason, and in the deepest parts of our hearts, we do believe that. But rational thoughts do not bring healing.

Here's the good news. God created us to exist entirely. Dealing with injured hearts, without healing, is not His plan for our lives. Christ came so that we, *"may have life and have it to the full"* (John 10:10, NIV). The world often taints our perception of "full." But God says, *"I do not give to you as the world gives"* (John 14:27, NIV). When God removes, rearranges, or changes our lives, He doesn't erase what was. He uses every experience He gives us to further His kingdom. Our pasts matter, and we have everything to show for the years we spent pursuing our dreams. We are no more for having experienced them and no less for having left them.

The enemy, however, wants us to feel invisible. He wants us to stay lost somewhere between agonizing over our loss and doubtful of God's goodness. This grey area is home to confusion.

But our Heavenly Father is not a God of confusion. He's a God of clarity and meaning.

Through these pages, I will reveal God's light as He shines truth on your hurt. You are God's sheep, and He says, *"My sheep listen to my voice; I know them, and they follow me"* (John 10:27, NIV). Your commitment to the Lord carries eternal value that not only saves you but those around you. God is using your past as a platform to broaden your reach. I invite you to stand firm as God reveals mysteries within your story. You are known, and you are loved. *I pray that the eyes of your heart may be enlightened in order that you may know the hope to which He has called you* (Ephesians 1:18, NIV).

Chapter 1

In My Dreams

Grabbing an old wooden bat, he headed towards the end of his gravel driveway that stretched out from his childhood home. Running his hands through the gravel, he cleverly chose the most prominent stones to send soaring through the air. Just beyond his driveway and nearby street lay a cornfield that held many of Josh's rocks. Without a moment's notice, he threw the rock into the air, swinging as hard as he could. The crack of his bat echoed across the yard as he watched the rock fly over the trees and into the field. Though it was only him and the roar of an imaginary crowd, each homerun lifted his imagination as he dreamed of playing the game he loved.

Within the borders of this small world lived a boy with big league dreams. He and his brother Jon often wore plastic baseball helmets while playing continuous whiffle ball games in their backyard. Josh's dad sometimes cut base paths out with his lawnmower, and the pool fence became the boys' homerun fence. They called the space "Kauffman Stadium," where homerun balls skyrocketed over the wall and into the pool. They cut MLB lineups out of the local newspaper and announced the game as they played. Each one of them represented his own MLB team hitting for each player in their lineups. Not only did they hit for each player, but they mimicked batting stances and other playing styles to bring the game to life. During these early years, Josh's love for the game was born. Over time it became his passion and dream in a world far away from the bright lights.

When Josh was a little league player, his dad bought him a new glove. After seeing it, Josh held it up to his nose to smell the new leather; but the closer he looked, he realized it wasn't like his brother's. The glove was for a left-handed athlete, which is exactly what Josh was. But wanting to be like his teammates, he asked his dad to buy him another one. Finally, his dad agreed to purchase a glove for a right-hander only because Josh promised to practice with his first glove before switching to a second. As a result, he used two gloves learning to throw with either arm.

Switch pitching became gradually aggravating for his opponents because Josh was able to throw no-hitters with either arm. On occasion, fans would argue with umpires regarding his ability. They believed it was against the league rules for an athlete to switch throwing arms within a single game. He always got away with it, though, because nobody found rules concerning the issue. Josh's little league coach got a kick out of the chaos and loved watching the opposing teams become unnerved. Using his right hand to throw a baseball is something Josh never abandoned throughout his career.

While in school, Josh never hesitated when his teachers asked him what he wanted to be when he grew up. He quickly responded each time by telling them he was going to be a Major League Baseball player. Of course, a lot of his friends uttered the same answer. You can imagine his teacher's reaction knowing that no one in the county's history had ever played in a Major League Baseball game. But that didn't stop Josh. He was a dreamer.

His teacher's first question was often closely followed with a second to the tune of, *What else would you like to do?* He never seemed to have an answer. As a young boy, Josh never thought there was a second option, or at least he was never able to come up with one. His dreams did not stop at the Pulaski County line; they stretched out across the country, filling every Major League stadium.

Josh grew up on Twin Oaks Farm in Eubank, Kentucky where life was simple. His parents raised him in a Christian home, and at the age of seven he accepted Christ as his Savior. What mighty and awesome plans God had in store for His child. There were dreams to dream and mountains to climb. If only Josh knew where God was going to take him! For such a child could not have possibly imagined the road he would travel or the impact he would make. His journey, though, would not begin without first being introduced to his helper. So not many years passed before the Lord brought me into his life.

I started dating Josh when I was sixteen. Truthfully, it's a miracle that we ever started dating. He was a ball of nervous energy around me, and I couldn't have been any more introverted. But I naturally gravitated towards him. He didn't pressure me to be someone I wasn't or do things I shouldn't. I loved that about him. But mainly his goofiness brought me out of my shell and allowed me to be myself.

Early in my junior year of high school, my friend told me that Josh liked me. He was supposed to call me but never actually followed through. Instead, I remember walking by him in the halls at school, exchanging glances and smiles. Every time I saw him, I began doubting what my friend had told me. I wondered if he would ever talk to me.

One day as I was leaving school, I began walking through the gymnasium when I caught Josh out of the corner of my eye. He was standing by the Coca-Cola machine, so I decided to go over and talk to him for the first time – which was entirely outside my nature. As he put money into the machine, I caught him off guard and nearly scared him to death. Fumbling around and losing his focus, he jammed his quarters into a random hole in the machine. Then, he began mumbling words about meaning to call me, and the longer he talked, the funnier he became. Let's just say by the end of the conversation he did not get a Coke! But that encounter is all it took. From that point forward he became my best friend.

Josh grew up with one older brother, like me, but I also had three younger sisters. My daily routine included fighting over food, hot water, and privacy. I tried to be an example to my sisters and did my best to help take care of them. As a result, I developed a deep sense of responsibility, leaving little space for dreaming. Honestly, my only dream before meeting Josh was earning a college degree and marrying a good Christian boy.

One could explain my knowledge of sports in four words: not enough to matter. I certainly didn't know anything about baseball. Oddly enough, I didn't even know Josh played baseball in high school. Up to that point, I only associated him with playing basketball. He started dunking as a sophomore which gained him a lot of attention from local fans.

But beyond the court was a baseball diamond that held his heart. In the first game I attended, Josh hit two home runs. I left thinking he must be pretty good. No matter how well Josh played, though, he always knew what I was doing. He'd wave at me or look over at me during the game. And afterwards he'd always ask me how my food tasted. How he could play and still know what I was doing was beyond me. That's another thing I loved about Josh. He wanted me to enjoy the game as much as he enjoyed playing it. Truthfully, I did. I'm not even sure it was the game I enjoyed as much as watching Josh do what he loved.

I learned that Josh hadn't always played centerfield. After pitching and playing shortstop for most of his younger playing years, he later moved to centerfield as a sophomore in high school. His coach needed to fill a void in centerfield and utilizing Josh's speed seemed most beneficial for the team. After making centerfield his rightful home, Josh further excelled at the game. His speed became most evident with his ability to track down fly balls and make diving catches. This single change in position transformed Josh into a stand-out, so much so that throughout his career he never returned to the infield again. His skills helped contribute to two regional tournament titles for the Pulaski County Maroons.

After hitting .522 as a senior with 10 home runs, 50 runs batted in, and 34 stolen bases, Josh desired to play baseball at the collegiate level close to home. His brother was attending Eastern Kentucky University and, knowing that it was only forty-five minutes from home, Josh's college choice became an easy decision.

Thankfully, he was able to attend EKU on a baseball scholarship but did so with an undecided major. During his uncertain academic path, one thing Josh was absolute about was his relationship with the Lord. As his dreams took flight, his faith kept him grounded. He was away from home and lost on campus, not knowing where his life was heading. Truthfully, baseball was the only reason he was at college, and this reality scared him. His lack of interest in other fields led him to cry out to God in desperation. While walking on campus as a freshman, he prayed and asked the Lord to have His way.

Josh understood he was incapable of figuring out life on his own.

From there, he gave himself entirely to his athletic gift while other people started taking notice. These people weren't only his coaches or teammates; they were people whose jobs included working for professional baseball organizations. During his junior year, professional scouts began coming to his games, watching his every move. They stood on the sidelines or behind home plate watching him hit, catch, and run. They began their study of Josh and what possible value he could bring to an MLB organization.

As a twenty-year-old junior, Josh set various single-season records, including runs (80), hits (106), singles (74), and stolen bases (57). In addition, Josh was EKU's first-ever first-team Louisville Slugger All-American after leading the nation with 57 stolen bases and batting .447--third best in the country.

As he continued to perform, it became clear to Josh that God was guiding him, and a pathway to achieving his dream was possible.

Letters and questionnaires began piling in from different MLB teams. Each letter Josh received took up residence in his heart. He placed them in a two-pocket folder along with their accompanying business cards. At night Josh would get this folder out and reread each letter to ensure they were real. He would stare at the MLB logos imagining himself playing for each team. While dreaming of a MLB career, he relentlessly practiced his autograph. Page after page of college notebooks were covered--not with lecture notes--but with his name. It was a name no one knew yet, but one I was getting ready to take as my own.

As his junior year began winding down, the reality of Josh getting drafted came into view. Unfortunately, I knew next to nothing about a baseball draft, so Josh had to do a lot of explaining. There were more than 40 rounds of draft picks by different MLB teams. Oh, and there were thirty MLB teams scattered across the country.

Teams were searching for their 2003 draft picks, and Josh understood his chances were favorable. The highest projected possibility for him was getting picked between the 1st and 2nd round or a 'sandwich' pick. But, of course, he didn't know for sure if he would get drafted that high. None of us did. But getting drafted at all meant we were getting married. I knew I would never leave home with Josh without a ring around my finger because the fear of God was in me, and the fear of my mom was in front of me.

The unknown was exciting and nerve-wracking. A part of Josh, deep down, didn't want to move across the country. I only say that because he truly loved being home. But he planned to go regardless of which team chose him. At least he wasn't traveling alone, because I was going with him. I didn't think much about moving, because at that point I had already lived in three different states. And the thought of having my own bathroom drew a smile from one end of my face to the other!

During the week of our wedding, I tirelessly worked in my childhood bedroom. Though I was only moving out of my parent's basement into Josh's parent's basement, a part of me wanted to cling to each picture and piece of clothing I packed. At the age of twenty, I was the first of five to leave home. Yes, I was transitioning ten minutes down the road, but in the back of my mind I knew that I would be traveling much farther than that.

While packing, I never mentioned any of that to my mom. I never asked her questions about living on my own or how to travel alone. I never asked her if she thought I would be okay or independent enough to make such a life-changing move. I was on a mission to check things off my to-do list. With that in mind, I continued packing my things. My drive to complete tasks was much like hers. She knew how to get things done. Together we worked without conversing about the certainty of what was happening. Her assistance seemed to answer my unspoken questions. She never once acted unusual or uneasy, which made me feel as though I would be fine.

Together we hauled out boxes filled with memories I would take with me. When the belongings dwindled to a few, I packed my arms with what remained. Holding a mound of clothing and hangers, I momentarily paused and glanced back. I stared at an empty room I remembered begging my mom for. I didn't receive my bedroom until I was thirteen after my mom and stepfather added more space in our unfinished basement. It was my little haven away from my siblings. Standing in the doorway, I saw the lavender paint that I picked out as a young teen. My yellow bedspread filled with daisies was all that stared back at me. It would be left for the next sister to occupy. After a few brief moments, I headed up the stairs and out the front door. I was unaware of the difficulty my mom had watching me leave, and she was unaware of the years she had spent preparing me.

Long before my wedding day, the Lord planted my mom's independent nature, strength, and faith within my soul. I never thought I wasn't ready for such a dramatic life change. Perhaps my age shielded me from such worries. But the truth was, the Lord *had* already prepared me for what was ahead.

God gives us talents and dreams. He also opens doors while closing others. Baseball was an open door for Josh, and together we boldly walked through it. While Josh's dream was playing baseball, my dream became marrying him.

On May 31, 2003, Josh and I promised each other and the Lord that we would stick together, no matter what happened. I assumed taking care of Josh wouldn't be too different from taking care of my younger siblings. And on our wedding day, he became my whole world. His goals became my goals, his victories were my victories, and his losses were my losses.

Three days after we said, "I do," Josh became the 119th overall pick selected by the Houston Astros in the fourth round of the 2003 MLB draft. Becoming an Astro meant we were headed to Troy, New York, for Josh to begin his professional baseball career. The Tri-City Valleycats was our first stop in Josh's climb to the Major Leagues.

Arriving in New York was somewhat comical. Neither one of us had ever been there before, and most people could figure this out the minute we started speaking. I don't think we could've outrun our "southernness" if we disguised ourselves and used voice changers. But honestly, we were relieved to make it to New York on our own without our parents. We felt like real adults.

Since neither one of us was twenty-one years old yet, the option of renting a car was out the back door. So, after our plane landed, a Houston Astros employee drove us to the park. My eyes widened when we pulled into the parking lot. I had never seen such a large stadium. Josh's heart was pumping out of his chest as he grabbed his bags and headed for the clubhouse. I took a seat in the stands and watched as he later ran across the perfectly manicured grass. For the life of me, I couldn't believe that baseball was my husband's job. Is that what I would tell people? The whole scene was surreal.

Josh was equally stunned. Seeing his name on his locker for the first time nearly took his breath. Of course, he tried to act normal to his new teammates, but there wasn't anything normal about it. Each of these players had found their yellow brick road, but we knew that not all of them would reach the big leagues. A baseball agent who represented Josh at the time told us that only a few players would make it. The rest were just there to help.

I desperately wanted Josh to be one of the few. One thing was sure: he wasn't backing down by any means. Josh gave everything he had to earn the respect of his teammates and coaches. This commitment required him to make several adjustments. He had to learn how to deal with failure while understanding that underperformance could end his dream. And I had to learn how to help him because I depended on him. By the end of his first professional season, Josh became a New York-Penn League All-Star.

In his climb to the big leagues, the next stop was a place that Josh's whole family was anxiously awaiting. Finally, in 2004, he became the first Kentuckian to play for the Lexington Legends. Many of his friends and family made the short trip to Lexington night after night to watch him play. He was living his dream as close to home as he would ever be. But it didn't last long.

While playing in the bluegrass state, he approached a game that still holds a special place in his heart. Most players do not focus on setting records, though this does occur for some of the athletes. Josh experienced this one Sunday afternoon in April. He tied a minor league baseball record by going six for six in a single game, scoring five runs, and stealing four bases. His success continued, and after playing in 73 games with the Legends, Josh batted .326 with 48 stolen bases. Midway through the season, he packed his equipment up, and we headed to Salem, Virginia. The Astros called him up to the next level.

The Lord opened yet another door, one that led closer to the Major Leagues.

Once joining the Salem Avalanche team, Josh had to continue making adjustments. With each move came new teammates, managers, and expectations. Josh constantly had to prove himself and his worth to gain playing time and his manager's confidence. At twenty-one years old, in his second professional season, he was still battling through growing pains. But his manager said something to him that year that was blunt and to the point. Staring at Josh, he told him that he had more talent in his pinky finger than some players had in their whole bodies, so he needed to start acting like it. Josh understood what his coach meant, and he worked on fine-tuning his skills. By the end of the season, he led all minor league baseball with 78 steals between Class A Lexington and Class A Salem. In addition, he was named a South Atlantic League All-Star and Postseason All-Star.

Being reminded of our gifts puts into perspective God's calling on our lives.

Josh spent the next two seasons in Corpus Christi, Texas, playing for the AA Hooks. The team was brand new, and in 2005, Josh was the first player in franchise history to step into the batter's box. That year Baseball America chose Josh as the Best Defensive Outfielder, and he led the Texas

League with 50 stolen bases. However, having to repeat the same league the following season was initially disappointing. Josh had worked very hard and had difficulty processing the reason why he needed to return to Corpus Christi. But he was grateful for the opportunity to continue living his dream and was more determined than ever to prove himself to the Astros organization. In 2006, the Hooks won the Texas League Championship. During the season, Josh recorded two five-hit games and stole 43 bases. He was the MVP of the Texas League All-Star Game, the MVP of the Corpus Christi Hooks team, and made the Postseason All-Star Team.

The 2006 Texas League Championship is the only title the Corpus Christi Hooks has won to this date. When we use our talents to help others succeed, we take part in something greater than ourselves. If Josh had not returned to Corpus Christi, he would have missed the opportunity to share in the team's most significant victory.

The following season Josh joined the AAA Round Rock Express in Round Rock, Texas. At this point, he was one call away from the Major Leagues. We both knew how close he was. This reality caused him to put an enormous amount of pressure on himself. One thing that kept us grounded was our unique living arrangement for the season. Normally we rented an apartment (even shared them with Josh's teammates), but this year we got to stay with a host family. They had a one-bedroom apartment on their property. Each day, we drove down their long driveway complete with cattle crossings to get to the baseball stadium. Being surrounded by longhorn cows reminded us of life at home on the farm.

Regardless of our temporary comfort, this season proved to be taxing on Josh. He knew how close he was to walking out on the field in a big league stadium, and mentally he battled with anxiety. Several players had big league experience, and Josh struggled to find his place among older teammates. The climate was vastly different from the previous season in Corpus Christi. Despite his struggles, he still managed to hit for a .273 average and steal 40 bases. Finally, in September, he received the call he had waited his whole life to hear.

On September 2, 2007, the Astros called Josh up to meet them in Chicago. I was pulling out of the HEB grocery store parking lot and was headed to Goodwill to drop off some donations when my phone rang. Josh's agent told me the good news, and I burst into tears. I then dialed Josh's phone and when he answered I couldn't get my words out. He kept asking me if I could believe it. Could I believe what was happening? No way! My head was swirling thinking about packing and getting an airline ticket for Chicago. When I pulled into the Goodwill parking lot to hand over my things, I had mascara running down my face. The attendant just stared at me and finally asked if I needed a receipt. Um, no. I shook my head and jumped back in my car thinking to myself, if only he knew what was happening!

Arriving in Chicago with Josh's parents was like stepping out of reality and into a movie. I always tried to imagine what it would be like to sit in the stands of a big league stadium and watch Josh live his dream, and here I found myself getting to do just that. Finding my seat, I sank down in a sea of Cubs fans waiting to catch sight of him. Others had made the same trip, including Josh's brother and wife, along with other extended family members. I even saw Josh's coach from EKU sitting a few rows behind us. What a day this was for all of us. When Josh finally came out of the guest dugout, I couldn't stop staring at him as he stood in line for the National Anthem. He achieved his dream, and no one could ever take that away from him. I was so proud of him and for all the years he worked to get there. But, more than anything, I literally witnessed God do the impossible.

The Lord gave Josh a natural gift and allowed him to use it at the highest level of baseball in the world. I praised Him for giving Josh his dream and allowing me to share in the experience. I, too, was given my dream: a Christian husband who loved me.

In the Bible, King David enters the Lord's presence and utters words that capture my exact feelings: *"Who am I, O Sovereign Lord, and what is my family, that you have brought me this far?"* (2 Samuel 7:18, NLT).

There were so many things to be thankful for the moment Josh took the field in Chicago. But, reiterating what King David asked, who were we that God would allow us to be in that very moment? Who was our family that they should share in our joy? I was overwhelmed with gratitude, believing that this was the beginning of a lasting career.

Like Josh, there may have been a time that you achieved your dream. So, let's take a moment to remember what God has done for us and what it means to walk and talk with Him.

A Prayer for Your Journey:

Thank you, Lord, for making the impossible possible. You have opened doors for me and allowed me the opportunity to experience my dream. There is no other God but you, and I give you all the praise. In Jesus' name, I pray, Amen.

A Hymn to Ponder:

In The Garden[1]

Written By: C. Austin Miles
Song By: Alan Jackson

I come to the garden alone,
While the dew is still on the roses;
And the voice I hear, falling on my ear,
The Son of God discloses.

And He walks with me, and He talks with me
And He tells me I am His own,
And the joy we share as we tarry there,
None other has ever known.

I'd stay in the garden with Him
But the night around me is falling;
But He bids me go; thro' the voice of woe,
His voice to me is calling.

And He walks with me, and He talks with me
And He tells me I am His own,
And the joy we share as we tarry there,

---

[1] "Alan Jackson - in the Garden (Live)." 2017.www.youtube.com. August 24, 2017. https://www.youtube.com/watch?v=hhIGIfsLxVk.

None other has ever known.

And the joy we share as we tarry there,
None other has ever known.

Chapter 2

Apart at the Seams

While with the Astros, Josh didn't play like a rookie. During September, with 67 at-bats, his batting average was .358. In addition, he reached base six times in a single nine-inning game, with five hits and a walk. This feat tied a 42-year-old record previously achieved by Joe Morgan. It was the most magical moment of professional baseball either one of us had ever experienced. Yes, there was pressure to perform, but Josh played his best, enjoying every single minute. Each night I waited on him to exit the clubhouse, and with my hand in his, we walked out of the stadium and down the street unnoticed by any passersby. It was him and me in a world far from Eubank, Kentucky. We reached the summit of our mountain and, for one brief moment, we embraced the awe-inspiring view.

But rather than being worked into the Astros' plans, they instead traded Josh to the Braves.

One afternoon in November, while Josh and his brother visited a farm in Wayne County, Kentucky, his phone started ringing. When he answered, the Astros told him he was no longer with the team. It felt like a sucker punch to the gut when Josh told me what happened. He had fought so hard at every level of the minor leagues with intentions of playing for the Astros. We somehow believed that his hard work and success would earn him a spot on the Astros' roster. But our naive thoughts had no place within the business deals of professional sports. Now with the Braves, Josh once again had to prove he was worth keeping.

Entering spring training in 2008, we both believed that Josh had a legitimate chance of earning a spot on the Braves' roster. Maybe with a new team, things would be different. Day after day he remained with the big league team and, as spring training came to an end, my hopes escalated. Josh was flying from spring training to Atlanta with the big league team to compete against the Cleveland Indians. As I kissed him goodbye, I realized that he had a watchful eye on the other players. Then he mentioned that there would be another roster cut because too many outfielders were boarding the plane. I refused to think negatively and told him not to worry because there was no way he would get cut. During the exhibition game in Atlanta, however, I sensed that something wasn't right.

Josh didn't come into the game until later, and the way he was playing made me believe that he knew something I didn't. By then I was used to watching him play. I could easily read his body language during a game. It turns out, while Josh was standing in the dugout, another player told him that he didn't make the big league team. Josh was going to get cut as soon as the game ended. So, when I saw him run across the diamond to the outfield, he already knew he wasn't staying. And sure enough, when the game was over, Josh's manager called him into his office and told him he would be playing for the Braves' AAA team in Richmond, Virginia. I was waiting outside the clubhouse with Josh's parents when he finally came out. I watched him walk towards me with his head down and I knew. When he finally looked up at me, he said that he was sorry. He didn't make the team.

This assignment to AAA caused Josh to obsess over his performance. More determined than ever to make an impact, he set a record hitting in 27 consecutive games and became the Richmond Braves Player of the Year. He hit .314 and stole 42 bases. As a result, he was called up to Atlanta once in May and again in late August. While with the Atlanta Braves that year, Josh hit .294 and stole ten more bases. His success earned him the Tommy Aaron Memorial Award for the Most Valuable Player.

By the following spring training we were excited to be with the Braves and, once again, believed that Josh had a real opportunity to break camp on Atlanta's 25-man roster. But this hope didn't last long. During a routine spring training game, the opposing pitcher for the Detroit Tigers was throwing a no-hitter when Josh came up to bat. He attempted to bunt which didn't settle well with the pitcher, especially since it was late in the game. But Josh was doing his best to show his skills with the goal of breaking camp with the Braves. Little did we know, he was getting ready to become the opposing pitcher's teammate. Within days of that game the Braves traded Josh to the Tigers. Before spring training ended, we packed up our things and drove from the Wide World of Sports to Lakeland, Florida.

At this point, I couldn't understand why teams weren't keeping Josh. By the end of the 2009 spring training, however, Josh found himself on the Detroit Tigers' 25-man roster. We were ecstatic and relieved when he broke camp with a big league team. It felt like he had made it for keeps after being traded twice. The Tiger's plans were to use Josh as a backup outfielder. So, he had to adjust to not playing every day, which was challenging to do. But we didn't question his role because he was still living his dream, even from the bench.

One July afternoon in Detroit, I sat on our couch in our apartment reading a Bible study called *The Virtuous Woman: Shattering the Superwoman Myth.*[2] I met with some of the other wives on the team periodically for this study and enjoyed what God was teaching me. That day, Josh had already left for the field to prepare for the evening game. When I turned to page 67 this scripture was at the top of the page:

He said to his disciples, "The harvest is great, but the workers are few. So pray to the Lord who is in charge of the harvest; ask him to send more workers into his fields."

—Matthew 9:37-38, NLT

At the time, I pondered on the truth of the scripture while not applying it to my life. Yes, I agreed God needed more workers, but I didn't ask Him to send me. As I continued reading, I got out my ink pen to underline important words. One such question caught my attention. *"Are we about the business He assigned us?"* I believed I was. Reading on, the last sentence on the page was worth underlining and putting a star by: *"Though the circumstances of our lives may change, our God-given purpose will remain steadfast for all times."*

I took my pen up to the top of the page because I wanted to rewrite that truth. So, I wrote, *"Though the circumstances of our lives may change..."*

Then, in mid-sentence, my phone started ringing.

---

[2] Courtney, Vicki. 2004. *The Virtuous Women: Shattering the Superwoman Myth.* Nashville, Tenn.: Broadman & Holman.

When I looked down and saw Josh's name, I grew a little anxious. So many times in the past when Josh called me after arriving at the stadium, it was to share news that changed his career trajectory. He rarely called just to check-in. After answering, he proceeded to tell me that the Tigers released him. I already learned that "released" was a fancy word for "thank you for your service, but you aren't needed any longer." But I couldn't believe my ears.

The Tigers placed him on waivers, which meant that any of the other 29 teams could pick him up. I wanted to deny reality because in my heart I believed Josh had finally found his place. He had value, and I knew the Tigers saw it. After all, they kept him on their roster out of spring training providing Josh with his first full season in the Major Leagues.

With my head swirling with questions, I stared down at my 36-week pregnant belly in silence. Baseball decisions used to only affect Josh and me, but now they involved our son. How could they do this to us? I grew weary from watching Josh get let down time and time again. He was as invisible as the wind. When the wind blows, we can see its power rustling through trees, scattering the earth, or drying the rain. But we can't physically see the wind. I felt at this point that, like the wind, no one could see Josh. He made an impact everywhere he went, but he himself was unseen.

Finally, I got myself up and drove to the Tiger's stadium to get Josh. When I arrived, I saw him standing outside the park like a spare tire strapped to the rear of a car. Very useful, but not needed.

Talk about circumstances changing. I never finished writing the sentence at the top of that page. Each time I see the space after the word *change*, my mind returns to the moment our lives were interrupted. Dreams don't come without obstacles, but we work harder to overcome them when we're allowed to try. Josh's opportunities were slipping through his fingers. But even acknowledging this reality, we still couldn't imagine our lives apart from his dream.

You may have experienced something like this before. Perhaps you have lost something you once had a tight grip on.

I cried out to the Lord during this time, praying, even begging Him to restore Josh's career. I pleaded with God to provide a team that would keep him. I couldn't understand why God would allow Josh to come so far without any assurance of a career.

The Kansas City Royals picked Josh up off of waivers and wanted him to join the team immediately. But we had traveled home from Detroit knowing that my due date was nearing. Understanding we both wanted Josh to be present at the birth of our son, my doctor scheduled a c-section after I underwent an amniocentesis.

In my 37th week of pregnancy, I gave birth to a healthy 9lb 10oz baby boy. I tried to prepare for Josh's departure because I knew he would leave as soon as our son was born. Less than 24 hours after giving birth, Josh kissed me and told me he would try and see Easton through the nursery window. It was four o'clock in the morning, and he was flying out to meet the Royals on a road trip. I was so tired that I barely acknowledged his goodbye, though I did tell him I loved him and would see him later. My only company at that point was a bouquet of flowers with a note that read, "Congratulations, love the Kansas City Royals." After Josh left, we didn't see him for two weeks.

I knew our time apart wasn't long, but it felt like an eternity because I longed to be with him. During this time, Josh was sorting through difficult emotions. He was with a new team and in a new city, again, without his family. When he called me at home, Josh often said that he sometimes forgot he was a dad. Those words devastated me because I couldn't stand not being there for him when I felt like he needed me.

There was one symbol, however, that brought him hope. While playing in the outfield at Kauffman Stadium, Josh could see a large cross in the distance on a hill. Staring at it, he took comfort in knowing God was with him.

Even so, the Royals did not have Major League plans for Josh. They did offer him a minor league contract that off-season, but someone else painted a more alluring scene. The Cincinnati Reds invited Josh to big league camp the following spring. He grew up watching the Reds, and when they called, he couldn't believe his ears. We couldn't imagine playing Major League Baseball within driving distance from home. Our family would be able to visit us, and so that settled our decision.

In 2010, after arriving in big league camp with the Reds, nothing about Josh's experience was as he anticipated. He thought he would have a better shot at making the Reds' roster, but several other outfielders were in camp to accomplish the same feat. Despite his efforts, Josh began the season playing for the Reds' AAA team called the Louisville Bats. He started the season in a slump, meaning he didn't perform well at all. It was the slowest start of his career. When he didn't get on base, he started pressing, which made things worse. His lack of performance earned him a seat on the bench where he wasn't put into games for days at a time. Josh couldn't explain the situation, and I couldn't bear to watch his career unravel. He had always had success despite changes made or the level of competition. I could not figure out what was happening, and I felt useless not being able to help him. If given time, however, I knew Josh would get everything sorted out.

But a few weeks into the season, the Reds released Josh. He then played for the Milwaukee Brewers AAA team in Nashville, Tennessee. A few weeks after that, the Brewers released him.

Then he headed to Gwinnett, Georgia, to play for the Braves' AAA team.

At this point, Josh told me something I had never heard him say before. He told me he wasn't sure if he was *supposed* to play baseball anymore. Not that he couldn't physically play, but did God want him to continue? Josh without baseball. Was that possible?

When we start to lose our dreams, our desires can fade with them. I watched as Josh's effort sucked the life out of him. Maybe if he tried harder, trained longer, or hit for more power, then his managers would've seen his potential.

But it didn't matter what Josh did because he couldn't stop the Lord's timing.

Then, in July, he broke his hand, which put him out for several weeks. Josh had never been seriously injured or put on any disabled list until that year. Shockingly, he didn't get the opportunity to recuperate and rejoin the team. On August 4, 2010, on our son's 1st birthday, the Braves released Josh.

Released.

Released.

Released.

Physically tired and emotionally drained, we packed our belongings and went home. I thought the magnitude of what happened would diminish if Josh were able to be around his family. But they couldn't understand what he couldn't explain.

Quite honestly, I was relieved to be home. In addition to having a one-year-old son, I was six months pregnant with our daughter. I knew our families could help us if we were near them. And Josh would be there with me. The pressure to perform was off his shoulders, but the unknown made him restless. His dream, or what was left of it, kept him from fully living. He was glad to be home but understood his career hung in the balance. Finally, after a few months, Josh received one last opportunity to continue chasing his dream. The Colorado Rockies offered him a minor league contract. And he accepted.

This time, the quick decision didn't settle well with either of us. But Josh said yes, knowing what that *yes* meant. He would be with another new team and forced to prove himself all over again. And having a toddler and a baby, I wasn't going to be able to travel out west with him to spring training. Monetarily speaking, we couldn't financially afford to go with him. No matter the reality, I still wasn't going to tell him not to go. Time apart wasn't a good enough reason for Josh to stay home, and I didn't want to be the reason his chase ended.

We began praying about the decision to sign with the Rockies but, truthfully, we already knew the answer. The Lord's Spirit within Josh was stronger than his grip on the game. We had no peace after previously saying yes. God has a way of doing that. Within days, Josh picked up the phone and made the most challenging call of his life. He told his agent that he wasn't going to accept the Rockies' offer. While his mind was determined to go, his heart said no.

Within a single moment, Josh gave up his dream.

The words fell off his tongue and hit the floor like a concrete block falling off a ten-story building. The damage was irreparable. And I had no idea how the weight of a few words could crush a person's spirit.

I hated that Josh had to make the final call. If only there hadn't been one last opportunity, we could have lived with the fact that Josh stopped playing because he *had* to. But that's not what happened. It was like putting out a fire, except Josh was the one spraying water. He extinguished the last opportunity he would ever have to play the game he loved.

In the days that followed, we both convinced ourselves that we had made the right decision and would make a new life at home together. But neither of us had any substantial reasons for being home. So, we didn't know what to tell his agent or our families. Why *were* we home? God must have had something for us that even we couldn't imagine. We believed that when one door closed, another one would open. Unfortunately, one major hurdle kept us from attaining this hope: there wasn't a door in sight.

Life at home grew increasingly unbearable. After a while, I stopped sending Josh to the grocery store. I'd send him to get milk, and he'd return two hours later. People stopped him and asked him about baseball everywhere he went. They had more questions than he had answers. Many told him not to worry because now he could be normal. Their good intentions brought anything but comfort. What did they mean by "normal?"

I faced the same questions. Once, while pumping gas, a man who recognized me began to ask about Josh. He wondered why Josh wasn't playing baseball anymore and then jolted me with a follow-up inquiry. As I tried to finish up and get home, he asked me if *Josh* had decided to quit playing. I stared at him, regretting my words as they came out. Yes, I told him, it was Josh's idea. But I knew it really wasn't. No one understood.

When no one understands what we can't explain, the absence of clarity can leave us lost and confused.

We knew the Lord wanted us home, but we didn't know why. So, to clarify our misunderstandings, we simply disguised our reasons in worldly phrases. We told people that we felt it was time for Josh to retire, or we believed it was time to switch gears. Both reasons dismissed the obvious, which was Josh was too young to retire, and he had no other passions in life to pursue. But I desperately wanted a good reason. For heaven's sake, I believe an injury would have brought me some comfort. At least no one would have questioned why we were home.

Another hurdle to jump over was the misperception of our reality. Yes, we were home, but we couldn't live happily ever after on what Josh earned while playing baseball. Josh desperately needed a job. But baseball was the only job he had ever had. I was starting to believe that his dream was costing us our future. Neither of us had finished our college degrees, and neither of us had "normal" job experience. It was all because of baseball. Our friends had worked several years into their careers, and we were standing there with little if anything to show. But most people assumed we were okay.

Waiting for clarity is excruciating when we're suffering in the present.

Like us, your immediate needs may be far louder than a hopeful restoration down the road-- especially if you can't see the road. In these moments, you may not even believe things will change in your favor. You didn't realize this heartache was coming. You have no Plan B because you didn't think Plan A would vanish. If God wants you to do something else, then why hasn't He made the way clearer? And why didn't He tell you ahead of time so that you could have prepared?

My mom asked me what Josh planned to do with his life. It was a logical question, but one I couldn't answer. Was Josh supposed to start applying for jobs everywhere in town? What were his skills? Did businesspeople care that Josh could steal bases when they were trying to sell cars? His résumé was dire, not to mention the fact that every other job on the planet paled in comparison to his dream. Yet, he couldn't perceive doing anything else. So, again, why were we home if there was nothing for us?

Days turned into weeks, and weeks turned into months. We didn't know what to do. Indeed, our children brought us joy, but no matter how hard we tried, we couldn't escape our past while trying to face the present. To make matters worse, pieces of Josh's dream were scattered throughout our home. No matter what corner we looked in, there were jerseys, bats, gloves, and pictures. They constantly reminded Josh of years spent pursuing his passion. His memorabilia painted a picture of who he used to be and suggested what he could have been had he stayed in the game. I realized his memories would never leave him. They woke him up each morning and tucked him in at night. No matter what I did, I knew I could never erase them.

When we lose that which we love, we grieve for our lost dreams that never die.

I grew to hate baseball during this time because of what it did to *my* dream. Josh wasn't the same as he once was. He stopped laughing, cracking jokes, and being goofy. Life lost its taste, and everything around us became bland. I wanted to cast his memories into the depths of the sea so they would no longer hurt him. But I agonized over the fact that I could never do that.

Dreams are not whiteboards that can be wiped clean. No, they are tightly knit sweaters that must unravel to remove their threads. Now that Josh's dream had come apart, emotions surfaced, causing him to suffer. If he complained about his situation, others might label him ungrateful, and if he yearned to pursue more in life, perhaps he was discontent. His solution, then, was to silence his feelings.

I watched as he smiled in public while his heart broke into a million pieces at home. That's where I spent my time sweeping to keep others from noticing his pain. But honestly, I did question whether or not he could ever be normal. Could he have a regular job? The kind where he'd wake up, put his time in, and then come home? The kind that wouldn't require him to make a diving catch or steal a base? More importantly, would he ever be able to enjoy anything other than his dream?

Seven months after saying no to his dream, Josh received a phone call from a dear friend. Greg asked Josh if he would consider joining the Fellowship of Christian Athletes ministry. The ministry served our local area and many other counties. This commitment required traveling, speaking, and mentoring athletes and coaches. At first, the job made logical sense for Josh because it combined ministry with sports. But when we read the fine print, I grew a little nervous. Josh would have to raise his salary to receive a paycheck.

Weren't people who raised support for a ministry called missionaries? Stating the obvious, I told Josh that we weren't missionaries. What bothered me the most was the lack of monetary help I could offer our family. With two young children at home, my full-time job was taking care of them. That meant that we all depended on Josh as we always had, but now it was different. He wouldn't perform to earn a paycheck; he would have to ask others to give to the FCA ministry to receive an income.

We still prayed about joining FCA, and though we didn't understand, we agreed that's where the Lord wanted Josh.

Little by little, as Josh poured himself out, the Lord poured Himself in.

But his healing didn't happen overnight. Josh dragged himself to church when he didn't want to go; he opened his Bible when he didn't feel like it; he attempted to pray when he didn't have words. He tried to follow the Lord when every inch of him resisted, because the lights behind him overshadowed the road ahead.

You may be able to identify with this same pain. Since you've picked up this book, I imagine that you've lost something that God gave you. I encourage you to hang in there with me as we travel this road together. Let's first consider what God has done.

Every good and perfect gift is from above, coming down from the Father of the heavenly lights, who does not change like shifting shadows.

—James 1:17, NIV

God is the giver of gifts, and He has blessed you and me with talents, skills, experiences, and relationships. Contemplate for a moment that God created us to share our stories with others. Our circumstances may have changed, but God hasn't. He did not suddenly decide one afternoon to rip your dream away, causing you years of hurt. Instead, God allowed you to choose between Him and your dream. And you chose Him.

When we choose God, He promises to remake us. We cannot cut out parts of His plan that we do not like or agree with because then we're only left with *our* plan. And that path is dark.

Deep down, under your hurt, I know there is a flicker of light that still shines for the Lord because you still love Him. You have walked with Him day after day, trusting He has your best interest at heart. And He does. But some decisions we make for Christ can be disappointing. I can relive Josh's phone call to his agent every day for the next fifty years and wonder if we made the right decision. I can also let our decision haunt me and make me feel guilty for not encouraging Josh to keep going.

But trusting the Lord with our choices means we have faith in His outcome.

Right now, the outcome may seem unbearable. One of your arguments could be that you chose God but not what you are currently doing. With all the uncertainty, you may have a list of reasons defending your opposition. For example, you may not feel qualified or experienced enough for what God has you doing. When you lived your dream, you had the confidence to excel in your craft. Now that your dream is gone, it's easy to believe that your skills went with it. Truthfully, you have other talents that you may not even know you have that God is bringing to the surface. Be encouraged to embrace what He's already prepared you for.

Forget the former things; do not dwell on the past. See, I am doing a new thing! Now it springs up; do you not perceive it? I am making a way in the wilderness and streams in the wasteland.

—Isaiah 43:18-19, NIV

God is doing something new in your life, and with your trust, He is making a way for you to accomplish His work. We must not dwell on what we can't change, but we can be thankful for what He has allowed us to experience.

During Josh's first year in FCA, student after student came to know Christ as their Savior. Do you know how Josh got their attention? Baseball. God already prepared him to enter the ministry. It was not an accident or because we made a wrong decision. That season of our life was intentional. Do you remember the cross I spoke about earlier? The one that brought Josh comfort while standing in the outfield at Kaufman Stadium? Unbeknownst to us, that cross was on the building of the FCA headquarters in Kansas City. That's not coincidental.

Your journey may have taken a turn, but you are not at a dead end. Take a moment to cherish the old rugged cross where Christ died to make accomplishing His work possible.

A Prayer for Your Journey:

Lord, you are the giver of gifts, and I thank you for the time I was able to enjoy my greatest passion. Please help me not to dwell on the past but to consider the new things you're doing. I chose you, and because I did, I desire to do your will. In Jesus' name, I pray, Amen.

A Hymn to Ponder:

The Old Rugged Cross[3]

Written By: George Bennard
Song By: Alabama

On a hill far away stood an old rugged cross,
The emblem of suffering and shame;
And I love that old cross where the dearest and best
For a world of lost sinners was slain.

So I'll cherish the old rugged cross
Till my trophies at last I lay down;
I will cling to the old rugged cross,
And exchange it someday for a crown.

O that old rugged cross, so despised by the world,
Has a wondrous attraction for me;
For the dear Lamb of God left His glory above
To bear it to dark Calvary.

So I'll cherish the old rugged cross
Till my trophies at last I lay down;
I will cling to the old rugged cross,
And exchange it someday for a crown.

To the old rugged cross I will ever be true,
Its shame and reproach gladly bear;
Then He'll call me some day to my home far away,
And forever His glory I'll share.

So I'll cherish the old rugged cross
Till my trophies at last I lay down;
I will cling to the old rugged cross,
And exchange it someday for a crown.
And exchange it someday for a crown.

---

3 "Alabama - the Old Rugged Cross (Live)." 2015.www.youtube.com. August 21, 2015. https://www.youtube.com/watch?v=MqKo_lsf5WY.

Chapter 3

Where's the Ram?

Josh didn't see a random cross, he saw something that was intentionally placed many years prior. The Lord gave him a glimpse of his future without him even realizing it. God says, *"I will instruct you and teach you in the way you should go; I will counsel you with my loving eye on you"* (Psalm 32:8, NIV). The Lord knows the way because He *is* the way. He is always preparing us and does so before changes in our lives occur. Josh was supposed to join the Royals, he was supposed to stand in centerfield, and he was supposed to see that cross.

When our lives unravel, however, sometimes we miss precious moments with the Lord when we blame ourselves for our misfortunes. We can argue that we made wrong turns, hasty decisions, or regretful choices. At what point will we trust our decisions made in faith? When will we believe that we are exactly where we are supposed to be?

Some of us never arrive at this place because the noise of the world chokes our ability to reason. Those around us have their opinions as to what we should have done or even the point of our lives that took a turn for the worst. This happened to Josh and me as well. Well-meaning people told us that we should have stayed in the Royals organization or that Josh should have signed with the Rockies because "you never know what might have happened." That's just it. We don't know what would have happened had we made different choices. But following Christ means He is in the lead, and our job is to trust Him as we say yes to this and no to that.

As Christians, we can pray for the Lord's will to be done, while simultaneously feeling cheated for having fulfilled it. Can't God just restore to us what He took? If He's testing our faith, then maybe He'll see our devotion and provide us a substitute as He did for Abraham.

Then God said, "Take your son, your only son, whom you love—Isaac—and go to the region of Moriah. Sacrifice him there as a burnt offering on a mountain I will show you."
—Genesis 22:2, NIV

Abraham was given a task unlike anything you and I have ever pondered. God told Abraham to sacrifice his only son whom he loved. God didn't tell Abraham to do it if he felt like it, or if he had time to do it. No, God told Abraham to do it. Can you believe Abraham got up the next morning after hearing from God and left? He didn't waste any time. How did Abraham even have the nerve to pack wood for the trip? As a mom, I feel physically ill at the mere thought. Imagine the conversation between Abraham and his son as they traveled.

Isaac spoke up and said to his father Abraham, "Father?"
"Yes, my son?" Abraham replied.
"The fire and wood are here," Isaac said, "but where is the lamb for the burnt offering?"
Abraham answered, "God himself will provide the lamb for the burnt offering, my son." And the two of them went on together."
—Genesis 22:7-8, NIV

Isaac was the lamb, unaware. He followed his father Abraham not knowing where they were going or his role in the sacrifice. When Abraham told Isaac that God would provide the lamb, Isaac accepted his father's guidance.

What if we, like Isaac, are the sacrifice?

Think for a moment about losses you have suffered. When faced with obstacles you couldn't maneuver around or mountains you couldn't climb, did you question God as to how your path would clear? Maybe He eased your confusion or anxiety by telling you He'd provide the tools you need to move forward. Or maybe He revealed to you that you are the tool. You are supposed to clear the way. You are to face uncertainty, pain, darkness, and discomfort in order to help others find their way. Will you follow through as Abraham did?

When they reached the place God had told him about, Abraham built an altar there and arranged wood on it. He bound his son Isaac and laid him on the altar, on top of the wood. Then he reached out his hand and took the knife to slay his son.

—Genesis 22:9-10, NIV

Abraham reaches his destination and continues without wavering. He arranged wood with his son beside him and then bound Isaac on top of it. Imagine looking down at your son tied to wood knowing his immediate death was your doing. Isaac trusted his father, who looked as if he was betraying him, and Abraham trusted God the Father, who looked as if He were betraying him. But Abraham trusted God prior to the sacrifice, and he trusted Him with the outcome. We aren't certain whether Isaac put up a fight or if he willingly allowed his father to restrain him. Either way, he complied. This act shows Isaac's devotion to Abraham and Abraham's devotion to God.

But the angel of the Lord called out to him from heaven, "Abraham! Abraham!"

"Here I am," he replied.

"Do not lay a hand on the boy," he said. "Do not do anything to him. Now I know that you fear God, because you have not withheld from me your son, your only son."

—Genesis 22:11-12, NIV

While Abraham was holding a knife above his son's body, God called out to stop what He initially told Abraham to do. How was God certain of Abraham's true devotion? Abraham didn't physically follow through with the sacrifice. Please take note of this: Abraham did follow through in his heart. God called Abraham to carry out a task and Abraham said *yes*. He prepared, traveled, built an altar, bound his son on top of it, and raised a knife over his body. God the Father is the only one who could have stopped Abraham. The mission was questionable, strange, and even incomprehensible. But Abraham never wavered.

For the word of God is living and active, sharper than any two-edged sword, piercing to the division of soul and of spirit, of joints and of marrow, and discerning the thoughts and intentions of the heart.

—Hebrews 4:12, ESV

God's Word is sharper than any knife Abraham could have carried. The Word divided Abraham's soul and spirit revealing the intention of his heart. And his heart was devoted. He was willing to sacrifice his only son that the Lord gave him.

Abraham looked up and there in a thicket he saw a ram caught by its horns. He went over and took the ram and sacrificed it as a burnt offering instead of his son.

—Genesis 22:13, NIV

God provided Abraham with a ram. It was a substitute that spared Abraham years of pain. I can't help but wonder after reading this encounter: Where is our ram? God is fully capable of giving us a substitute, so why hasn't He?

Knowing the Lord can provide us a way out is one way of thinking and making space for the possibility that He doesn't is another. God's outcomes all have unique purposes. It was meant for Abraham to have his ram, and it is meant for us to follow through with God's mission. Abraham had a substitute, but many of us *are* the substitute.

God sees the intentions of our hearts and that is why He has chosen us. He is not calling us to do something that He hasn't already done. You may have already accepted what God has called you to accomplish or experience but are holding on to the idea that someone else will pick up the weight of your cross. Or better still, maybe your load will lighten, lessen, or altogether disappear. Does faithfulness count for something? Yes, faithfulness always matters, but it's not a substitute. You can be faithful with pain and be faithful without it. The point is, are you willing to carry out what God has in store for you? We can't agree to God's plan and slowly grudge ahead waiting on Him to spare us. He wants to see His plan carried through to completion for our benefit (Philippians 1:6). God finishes everything He starts. We can join Him, or we can bail out. Either way, we must accept that His plan may include suffering.

One Biblical character who understands suffering is Job. He suffered from losing everything he held dear and the ability to see God's reasons for his loss. The Bible describes him as innocent and honorable. *He feared God and stayed away from evil* (Job 1:1, NLT). Though respectable, God also describes him as *the greatest man among all the people of the East* (Job 1:3, NIV). That means he was very wealthy. When God allowed Satan to afflict Job, he lost his family, everything he owned, and his health was at risk. Job didn't accuse God of wrongdoing, but he did verbalize thoughts that you and I can understand.

"What I always feared has happened to me. What I dreaded has come true. I have no peace, no quietness. I have no rest; only trouble comes."
—Job 3:25-26, NLT

Job says he has no peace, and he has no rest. He doesn't have any peace because he lost everything, and he can't rest because he knows that he can't change it. His words illustrate something has happened. Job's familiar walk with God has been tampered with, which terrorizes his mind and soul.

Is experiencing the goodness of God temporary? Even though you and I enjoy His blessings, many of us still fear they won't last. Sometimes we don't believe we initially deserved them. But we dismiss these negative thoughts to prevent polluting our faith. If we consider the possibility of losing our dream, however, then why don't we plan for a different scenario? It's simple. We don't want our lives to change. If God saw fit to give something to us, then why would He remove it? Here, Job's words drive through our hearts like daggers. He experienced what he most feared--losing what he enjoyed. Thankfully, he had a relationship with the Lord. This foundation prevented him from blaming God, but it didn't stop his hurt from leaking out.

"But I don't have the strength to endure. I have nothing to live for. Do I have the strength of a stone? Is my body made of bronze? No, I am utterly helpless, without any chance of success."
—Job 6:11-13, NLT

Job begins to question himself. He says that he's not strong enough to deal with what is happening, and he can't help himself when everything around him has dissipated. When you lose your dreams, everything you've worked for, your resources can disappear as well. When what you once depended on and lived on is lost, it's hard for you to strategize your next step. How can you pay your bills? How can you support your family? How can you start over if you have nothing?

When my husband turned down his last baseball offer, we believed in our hearts that because we followed the Lord's calling that He would immediately provide a new occupation or way of making an income. Well, days turned into weeks, and weeks turned into months. There weren't any jobs available for Josh. Not only did he struggle in finding work, but his patience held him hostage to try anything new. Should he work for a local business, or should he continue waiting on God to provide clarity while not making ends meet? Every other job felt wrong, and Josh felt misplaced. When we feel like we don't belong anywhere, our decision to leave what we love mirrors sabotage. Job makes this clear below.

"Your hands shaped me and made me. Will you now turn and destroy me? Remember that you molded me like clay. Will you now turn me to dust again?"

—Job 10:8-9, NIV

God took time to create Job by shaping and molding him like clay. When moist clay is left alone it dries out and becomes brittle. Life without purpose is like dry clay. It's hard, cracks easily, and isn't very useful. Most of us would throw meaningless clay in the trash. Why keep what we can't use? Like us, Job wants God to remember His creation, the one He fashioned and breathed life into. But it's hard to find a spark of meaning when our losses once painted for us a portrait of purpose. Where is our worth when the weight of God's call is turning us to ashes?

Think about this for a moment. Job is described as the greatest man of the East for a reason. He couldn't have earned such a description on luck alone. No, he would have worked very hard, and he would have had help. The Lord provided the means for Job's successes. Job was accomplished, and he understood why. So why did he have to suffer? Let's look at what Satan had to say.

"Does Job fear God for nothing?" Satan replied. "Have you not put a hedge around him and his household and everything he has? You have blessed the work of his hands, so that his flocks and herds are spread throughout the land. But now stretch out your hand and strike everything he has, and he will surely curse you to your face."

—Job 1:9-11, NIV

We know that Job didn't curse God because scripture states, *In all this, Job did not sin in what he said* (Job 2:10, NIV). Take a step back and look at these scriptures from God's point of view. I find Him incredible for accomplishing multiple purposes. First, Satan got the opportunity to acknowledge God's power. And he did! Satan verbally admitted that God protects His children, and He blesses them. Then, God teaches the enemy a lesson. Satan can try his best to destroy God's children, but they won't turn from Him when they are committed. God chose Job to reveal true love and devotion to an enemy who daily mocks such faithfulness. Job was also chosen for you and me. When we stay the course, purpose will emerge from our loss and that is where we find our worth.

Take note of this truth. Being separated from your dream doesn't mean you've separated from God.

Jesus shouted to the crowds, "If you trust me, you are trusting not only me, but also God who sent me. For when you see me, you are seeing the one who sent me. I have come as a light to shine in this dark world, so that all who put their trust in me will no longer remain in the dark."
—John 12:44-46, NLT

Do you know why Jesus shows us a connection here between Himself and the Father? They are one. Christ's death on the cross fulfilled the Father's plan, but it didn't create division in their unity. Jesus trusted the Father despite the pain and suffering He endured. If you stay committed to the Father's plan for your life, you acknowledge your love for Him and your devotion to complete His mission. He is your light, and because you believe in Him, you do not have to walk in darkness.

Our commitment, however, doesn't equal a comfortable life. God never said, "If you follow me, I'll give you every single thing you want." He does say, *Take delight in the Lord, and he will give you the desires of your heart* (Psalm 37:4, NIV). I know what you're thinking. God took away your desires when you were delighting in Him. Now you sense betrayal in your relationship with Him. Desires are things you and I want very strongly, and as Christians, our main desire must be to follow Christ and do His will. The desires of our hearts will become God's desires as we take pleasure in Him.

Yearning for the Lord more than our dreams gives us the ability to wait for His logic to unfold. In this transition, the Lord helps us be open and flexible to what He has planned for us.

During Josh's baseball career we were used to making decisions very quickly. The game of baseball may appear to move slowly through the eyes of onlookers, but the business side is aggressive. When Josh was presented with baseball offers, he usually had 24 hours to decide--if that. Our prayers were prayed with urgency. Then, one day when baseball ended, our world came to a complete stop. We were sitting at home twiddling our thumbs, and the pace was unnerving. We wanted answers quickly but were unable to attain any.

It's important to note that as we consider what God is doing, He may not give us many details upfront. Let's reconsider His servant, Abraham.

Now the Lord said to Abram, "Go from your country and your kindred and your father's house to the land that I will show you." So Abram went, as the Lord had told him, and Lot went with him. Abram was seventy-five years old when he departed from Haran.

—Genesis 12:1,4, ESV

God told Abraham to leave his home, his people, and his family to a place that God would show him. Abraham had no idea where he was going. Did the Lord have a beautiful house waiting on a hill for Abraham encircled with a white picket fence? No. What was in it for Abraham? Nothing that he could see. But he listened to God's voice and followed. We have no record of his thoughts, but considering he was seventy-five years old, leaving home was a bold move. This account teaches you and me that God may ask us to leave what He's given us for an unknown reason, and He may call us at an age that appears inconsistent with the task.

Remember, our flexibility helps us cope with changes in our lives. Where God calls us is where He's waiting for us. If we choose to stay where He's not, we are choosing to walk in the dark.

"Whoever walks in the dark does not know where they are going."

—John 12:35, NIV

You have no way of knowing the challenges or uphill battles that lay ahead. Apart from the Lord, you have no way of overcoming them either. In the life of a believer, that's reason enough to act because we understand that apart from God, we can't do anything (John 15:5). As hurt as we are for losing our dreams, let's think about our lives without the loss. Yes, we would have continued living out our dreams, but we would have done so without progressing in our faith. That scenario is not in our best interest. We can't attain a deeper relationship with the Lord without exercising our faith.

Prioritizing your relationship with the Lord above your fleshly desires allows Him to mold you like clay. As a result, you're able to shape into His likeness.

Becoming more like Christ means that worldly success is not our aim. Yet, some people still choose their plans, knowing their decision is apart from God. They sacrifice God's light to walk in darkness. God knows our hearts, and He knows what holds us back. I have no doubt you were doing the Lord's work when you were living your dream. But consider how He may use you more effectively by doing something new.

Josh worked very hard to get to where he was, and he gave God all the credit. That is what hurt me the most. Why would God take something from someone who loved Him? I agonized over this reality as Josh's career slipped further and further out of his reach. When we have a tight grip on something the Lord wants to change, He can allow our situations to become so dire that letting go is our only option. Could Josh have continued playing? Yes. But not without a fight. During that time, one of Josh's teammates asked him an important question: "Are you willing to fight to stay in the game?" In other words, how bad do you want this? The truth is Josh had been fighting for years to get to where he was. Fighting wasn't the issue; surrendering was.

Again, whose business are we concerned with? God says, *"For my own sake, for my own sake, I do this. How can I let myself be defamed? I will not yield my glory to another"* (Isaiah 48:11, NIV). Our dreams cannot overshadow the Lord, no matter how much they mean to us. Not when we have surrendered to Him. Even though Josh's drive to play professional baseball birthed out of his passion for the game, the world likes to portray a different rationale. Professional sports taunt young athletes with the possibility of fame and wealth. Josh didn't have either; he only wanted to use his gift to earn a living. But no matter the motive, someone would have always put him on a pedestal no matter how many times he knocked it over. It's the perception that someone in that position is above others. That attention competes daily with God.

Dreams often put us in a bubble, altering our sense of reality. But when we surrender to the Lord, He takes the attention directed towards us and uses it for our good and His glory. If we allow Him, He will use our past experiences to accomplish His purposes. They become a platform to point others to Christ.

Josh accepted the opportunity to work for FCA as an area representative. His work ethic and drive to perform transferred to his new position as a missionary. He wanted to tell every young person he knew about Jesus and was determined for the Lord to shine brighter than his baseball career. He spoke with countless youth groups, sports teams, coaches, schools, and churches. Josh said yes to nearly every single speaking opportunity and poured himself out like a drink offering. He didn't know any other way. Spare moments only became minefields for his mind to wander while the temptation to look back continuously gnawed on his spirit.

And there again, was no ram, or way out of his decision.

Choosing the Lord may mean no one will remember what we did, and no one will acknowledge what we currently do. This reality is the most significant slice of humble pie we will ever eat. Each morning we must wash it down with a tall glass of, "Lord, please help me to accept the things I cannot change."

But the Lord keeps every detail of our stories intact. He doesn't want us to act as if He never gave us our dreams. He has provided us with experiences unknown to others, and He desires for us to share them. Through our hurt, let's not dismiss what He's done. Our past has taught us lessons that others need to hear.

Out of Josh's despair, he looked at me one afternoon and asked if I thought Jesus' disciples ever thought about fishing. His question caught me off guard because I knew several disciples were fishermen. Of course, they probably thought about it. As he continued to speak, I began to understand what he was implying. He said that some of the disciples were fishermen. Fishing was their job, and they were good at it. Then one day, they dropped their nets after Jesus called them away. After choosing to follow Christ, did they think about fishing?

As Jesus was walking beside the Sea of Galilee, he saw two brothers, Simon called Peter and his brother Andrew. They were casting a net into the lake, for they were fishermen. "Come, follow me," Jesus said, "and I will send you out to fish for people." At once they left their nets and followed him.

—Matthew 4:18-20, NIV

All at once, they left their nets and followed Christ. We read that sentence as if their decision was effortless. Did they even know what Jesus meant by "fish for people?" I can't imagine they did. There must have been questionable days where they thought about their former lives. And there will be days where we'll do the same. Following the Lord, however, provided the disciples first-hand accounts of the greatest story ever told. It's a story that you and I can become a part of.

In our journey, let us hold unswervingly to our faith and not flee where God has led us. It's easy to think about our pasts, but no matter how dry and desolate our current scenery is, our commitment has brought us to this place.

We do not have a ram, because one isn't needed.

With each small step of faith, allow God's truth to light your path. Like Josh, you've already fought for your dream, and now it's time to drop your net. Regardless of your strength, the Lord will help you every step of the way.

A Prayer for Your Journey:

Lord, I'm tired and worn out. It's hard to surrender something that I love especially when you gave it to me. I pray you will help me give up my dreams and hurts along with every inch of me that you took time to mold and shape. I know that apart from you, Lord, I will never be able to do what you've called me to do. In Jesus' name, I pray, Amen.

A Hymn to Ponder:

Worn[4]

Song By: Tenth Avenue North

I'm tired
I'm worn
My heart is heavy
From the work it takes to keep on breathing

I've made mistakes
I've let my hope fail
My soul feels crushed
By the weight of this world
And I know that You can give me rest
So I cry out with all that I have left

Let me see redemption win
Let me know the struggle ends
That You can mend a heart that's frail and torn

I want to know a song can rise
From the ashes of a broken life
And all that's dead inside can be reborn
'Cause I'm worn

I know I need
To lift my eyes up
But I'm too weak
Life just won't let up
And I know that You can give me rest
So I cry out with all that I have left

Let me see redemption win
Let me know the struggle ends
That You can mend a heart that's frail and torn

---

[4] "Tenth Avenue North - Worn (Official Music Video)." 2013.www.youtube.com. March 13, 2013. https://www.youtube.com/watch?v=zulKcYItKIA.

I want to know a song can rise
From the ashes of a broken life
And all that's dead inside can be reborn
'Cause I'm worn

And my prayers are wearing thin
I'm worn even before the day begins
I'm worn I've lost my will to fight
I'm worn so heaven come and flood my eyes

Let me see redemption win
Let me know the struggle ends
That You can mend a heart that's frail and torn

I want to know a song can rise
From the ashes of a broken life
And all that's dead inside can be reborn
Yes, all that's dead inside will be reborn
Though I'm worn
Yeah, I'm worn

Chapter 4

What I Never Did, Is Done

Josh's decision to leave the game he loved paralyzed him for many years. What might have happened had he stayed in the game of baseball? Perhaps nothing notable. But what if he would have set records, won a gold glove, or made a big league all-star team? His commitment to follow Christ meant that he would never know the outcome of staying, only the pain of leaving.

There was no going back. Whatever Josh didn't do in baseball was done.

He decided to leave.

He completed his training.

He finished his career.

Some decisions we make only affect a moment. Others, however, can change the rest of our lives. Pain comes when we can't undo what's been done. How can we possibly move forward when our decision made in faith crushes our spirit? Life can be depressing when we can't get excited about a new season. This brokenness prevents us from embracing anything else God has in store for us because we've already devoted our time, spent our energy, and consumed our resources. Thankfully, the Lord shows us how to move forward.

Jesus came to a place in time where there was nothing left for Him to do except follow through. Did Christ question what would have happened if He stayed on earth a little longer? No. It was time for Him to move on. His mission was to save the whole world, which meant He had to leave His creation to do so. Christ knew when His task was complete. So did Josh. And so may you. But Jesus prepared Himself to follow through with His decision. We need to do the same. Pay attention to what He says and does in the following scriptures.

Later, knowing that everything had now been finished, and so that Scripture would be fulfilled, Jesus said, "I am thirsty." A jar of wine vinegar was there, so they soaked a sponge in it, put the sponge on a stalk of the hyssop plant, and lifted it to Jesus' lips. When he had received the drink, Jesus said, "It is finished." With that, he bowed his head and gave up his spirit.

—John 19:28-30, NIV

Just before surrendering His spirit, Jesus said He was thirsty. Imagine Christ's body nailed to the cross, covered in blood. He was poured out like water and all His bones were out of joint (Psalm 22:14). Yet in His last moments, Jesus said He was thirsty. Why would He say that? He said this to fulfill scripture and to model behavior that we should imitate. Remember, Jesus is our Savior, and He is also our teacher. He teaches us with every action He performs and with every word that He speaks.

Jesus quenched His thirst as a concluding act leading Him into a new season. He prepared Himself to die in order to save that which is lost. To emulate this behavior means we must thirst for Christ, or we'll never be able to die to ourselves and fulfill what He's called us to do. Earlier in the book of John, Jesus sheds light on this act.

On the last and greatest day of the festival, Jesus stood and said in a loud voice, "Let anyone who is thirsty come to me and drink. Whoever believes in me, as Scripture has said, rivers of living water will flow from within them." By this he meant the Spirit, whom those who believed in him were later to receive. Up to that time the Spirit had not been given, since Jesus had not yet been glorified.

—John 7:37-39, NIV

We can all relate to what it feels like to be thirsty. Thirst is caused primarily by dehydration. Many of us turn to water to cool ourselves down or rehydrate. Imagine, for a moment, being stranded in a hot desert for hours. The sun is beaming down on your face, and your mouth becomes so dry that you can barely open and close it. Would you, in the scorching heat, look for water? Of course you would. What if the water you needed was right beside you?

Sadly, many of us complete a mission and then hang our heads without ever seeking the Lord for a drink from His Spirit. We can't move forward because our spirits are weak. But the Lord shows us how to regain our strength. After He took a drink, He gave up His spirit so that you and I can receive it when we come to Him. The Spirit is our Comforter. Jesus wants us to come to Him so that He can comfort us. Our spirits cannot survive without Him. God makes this clear in the Old and New Testaments.

...man does not live on bread alone but on every word that comes from the mouth of the Lord.

—Deuteronomy 8:3, NIV

In this reference, God is speaking to the Israelites. He reminds them that He is their provider and caretaker regardless of their situations. They had been in the desert for 40 years, relying on God to feed them. He humbled them, and when they were hungry, He fed them. How does one find enough food in the desert to feed thousands of people? It's not possible with man. But God performed the miraculous. The people needed every morsel of food God gave them to survive, and they needed to obey every word He spoke to live. Life in the desert wasn't about eating bread; God's lesson taught the people to trust the One providing the bread.

The Lord then repeats Himself in the New Testament:

"It is written: 'Man shall not live on bread alone, but on every word that comes from the mouth of God.'"

—Matthew 4:4, NIV

In this second reference, Jesus speaks these words to Satan. After fasting for 40 days and 40 nights, Satan tempted Jesus in a most fragile moment. Think about how hungry Christ must have been when Satan approached Him. What did the enemy say first? He told Jesus that if He was the Son of God, He should turn some nearby stones into bread. I can't imagine the restraint needed to leave the stones as they were when Christ was hungry. But He didn't give in. He told the enemy that man doesn't live on bread alone but on every word from God. He said this for our benefit.

If bread can only temporarily sustain us, what do we expect from our dreams? Only God can enable us to live (Acts 17:28).

Deciding to follow God's calling in your life is a harrowing one when you are spiritually hungry. Temptation may cause you to seek answers or comfort elsewhere, but the Lord reveals the necessity for us to go to Him. He is the author of life itself (Acts 3:15).

When Josh began sharing his testimony, many people came forward to put their faith in Christ. The Spirit moved in their lives, and they started a new relationship with Jesus. As they made this decision, they did so without seeing the pain that Josh was in. The core of his hurt was spiritual hunger. He was doing what the Lord asked while starving in the process. But Josh's pain-filled choice to leave his dream allowed others the opportunity to choose Christ.

Just as we sometimes overlook the pain of those around us, sometimes we take Christ for granted, not contemplating the pain He endured. It's easier to imagine Jesus in heaven rather than hanging on a cross. Can you imagine witnessing His death? What if you were His earthly mom? Consider the horrifying scene. And to think that there were people there who approved of such torture. There were people present who were pleased to see Jesus die. When Jesus gave His final breath, these onlookers simply turned away from the one who died for them. Rejecting Christ meant that they also rejected the Spirit. They denied salvation and the opportunity to receive sustaining comfort.

When we lose our dreams, the world appears to rejoice as we grieve. We grieve for our losses because we can't make sense of the despair that follows. In our pain, it's possible to act as onlookers, rejecting the only one who can comfort us. Jesus warned His disciples of this exact situation before He died.

Jesus went on to say, "In a little while you will see me no more, and then after a little while you will see me."

—John 16:16, NIV

The disciples didn't understand what Jesus was telling them. They kept asking each other what He was talking about. Jesus saw them and knew they were confused so He explained His words to them.

"Are you asking one another what I meant when I said, 'In a little while you will see me no more, and then after a little while you will see me?' Very truly I tell you, you will weep and mourn while the world rejoices. You will grieve, but your grief will turn to joy. A woman giving birth to a child has pain

because her time has come; but when her baby is born she forgets the anguish because of her joy that a child is born into the world. So with you: Now is your time of grief, but I will see you again and you will rejoice, and no one will take away your joy."

—John 16:19-22, NIV

The disciples were going to lose Jesus in the flesh, but their pain wouldn't last forever. God tells us that women have pain in childbirth because their time has come, but after seeing their babies, they forget their anguish. What occurs between a woman's labor starting and her holding her baby? Pain. Some women's pain lasts longer than others. Those who have lost their dreams can relate to this scenario. When our time has come, and we let go of what we love, we experience pain. Some of us feel this heartache for many days, others for months, and many more for years.

Your time of grief might be right now. Notice that Christ says He will see you again and, when He does, you will rejoice! I believe this scripture refers to when we see Jesus face to face, but you will also rejoice when you see purpose emerge from your commitment to Christ on Earth.

And when you see Him in your purpose, no one can take away your joy. The key is not to reject Him in your sorrow.

Weeping and mourning are genuine emotions that occur after a loss or change. In these moments, the world still turns, and people carry out their lives around us without realizing the agony we're in. Then, to add gasoline to the fire, some people live out our dreams right in front of us. That's hard to grasp, because we know there is nothing we can do to change our circumstances.

Josh experienced this every time he turned on the TV to watch a baseball game. Often, he never watched a complete game, just bits and pieces. He wanted to be where his friends were but knew he never would. Unfortunately, I never fully understood the extent of His torment because I was trying to keep moving forward. I wanted us to look like a typical family with ordinary jobs, and in the process, I sometimes overlooked the hurt Josh experienced. He was like a caged thoroughbred wanting to run his race but could only watch others do so from the sidelines.

The one thing he never said out loud was the one thing that ate him alive from the inside out. He *had* what it took to play professional baseball because God had given him the ability, but he couldn't continue playing because God didn't want him to. This agony is the equivalent of *"In a little while you will see me no more..."* (John 16:16, NIV), because the Lord removed His hand from Josh's career. Neither of us could make sense of what happened. Darkness came over us in those moments, preventing us from seeing Jesus because the mission, or Josh's career, was complete.

Even Jesus Himself understands this feeling. As He was preparing for His death, He cried out to the Father, questioning His presence.

From noon until three in the afternoon darkness came over all the land. About three in the afternoon Jesus cried out in a loud voice, "Eli, Eli, lema sabachthani?" (which means "My God, my God, why have you forsaken me?").

—Matthew 27:45-46, NIV

Bearing the sins of the world, Jesus felt separation from His Father. Darkness encircled Him just as darkness can encircle us when we do what the Father has called us to complete.

During this time of uncertainty, we need to ask the Father for a drink, so that after a little while we will see Him again. We will see His hand at work in our commitment to follow through with His specific will for our lives. And this clarity will come because the Spirit reveals truth (John 16:13).

But what about the moments in between?

When we can't see or make sense of what the Lord is doing in our lives, a natural reaction is to turn away from the uncertainty towards what we can visualize--the past. It's simple for us to wallow in the past like a pig taking a mud bath. Though it may feel soothing, we will most certainly need cleansing. In the past, we lived our dreams, did what we loved, enjoyed a sense of purpose, and worked to accomplish goals. The past lights are bright for many of us, and we can see for miles down the road simply by turning around.

But the truth is, we aren't supposed to dwell on our pasts at all because God is always doing something new (Isaiah 43:18-19).

I felt just as confused as Josh did. Looking back for me meant seeing myself as Josh's wife and helper during his career. That was it. I didn't personally see any other purpose in my role. Looking forward, the only difference I could visualize was motherhood. But the path in front of me was dark. Where was it leading me? Besides Josh making a new life for himself, what was I supposed to do? Josh's gifts were evident, but mine were as bleak as a grey sky on a rainy day. I sure hoped that God was doing something new, because I couldn't perceive a place to be useful outside of being a mom.

When I couldn't see the Lord's direction, I did the only thing I knew to do, which was take care of my two children and continue to be Josh's helper. I hadn't finished the college degree I started, so I knew there were jobs that I couldn't apply for. And at the same time, I knew childcare costs would outreach any potential income. So, I felt stuck and helpless in many ways.

If you have ever felt this way, you will relate to Mary Magdalene. After Christ died on the cross, He appeared to several people. One of them was Mary Magdalene. In John Chapter 20, scripture says she went to the tomb and saw that the large stone had been removed from the entrance. Realizing Christ was gone, she went directly to a couple of Jesus' disciples and explained what happened. Jesus was not in the tomb but taken. The two disciples she was speaking to ran back to the grave only to discover that she was right--Christ was gone.

Then the disciples went back to where they were staying. Now Mary stood outside the tomb crying. As she wept, she bent over to look into the tomb and saw two angels in white, seated where Jesus' body had been, one at the head and the other at the foot.

—John 20:10-12, NIV

Imagine how distraught Mary was when she couldn't find Jesus. But then, she saw two angels, and they began speaking to her.

They asked her, "Woman, why are you crying?"
"They have taken my Lord away," she said, "and I don't know where they have put him."
At this, she turned around and saw Jesus standing there, but she did not realize that it was Jesus.

—John 20: 13-14, NIV

Mary was confused and heartbroken because Jesus was gone. It was a terrifying time for her. But during her time of uncertainty, where *was* Jesus? He was right beside her. Mary went as far as she could, then stayed where she was. She tried using her logic, even speaking with others (in her case, angels), when all along Jesus was standing beside her. Watch what happens when He speaks to her.

He asked her, "Woman, why are you crying? Who is it you are looking for?" Thinking he was the gardener, she said, "Sir, if you have carried him away, tell me where you have put him, and I will get him."
—John 20:15, NIV

Mary was speaking to Jesus and didn't even realize it. Do you know why? She was using her logic to bring about clarity. Notice when she said, *"...I will get him."* In other words, you give me what I need, and I will figure this out.

Have you ever talked to God like this before? I know I have. It seems so innocent. Sometimes we try to go about our business without bothering God. We may feel that we can solve our problems within our means. If He could just give us a tad bit of information, then we'll be good to go. We'll be able to piece our broken lives back together. Doing this sends a message to the Lord that we don't need all of Him, just a piece of what He's willing to give.

But *all* of Him has already died on the cross for us. He's already given His entire self to save humankind.

Let's go back to the moment Mary was talking to the Lord. She was in His presence and didn't see Him. I've often heard people say that God has never spoken to them. Could it be that He has, but their minds were preoccupied with questions, sadness, or grief? They were searching for Jesus, even speaking to Him, but could not hear because of their inability to be still and listen. Instead of believing we are *stuck*, look what happens when we become *still*.

Jesus said to her, "Mary."
She turned toward him and cried out in Aramaic, "Rabboni!" (which means "Teacher").
—John 20:16, NIV

Mary sees Jesus when He speaks her name. She provided space for the Lord to say something very intimate. There's nothing more cherished than hearing the Lord speak directly to you. And nothing sheds more light than listening to His voice.

Our own logic will never shine enough light to clear confusion or mend broken hearts.

Trust in the Lord with all your heart and lean not on your own understanding. In all your ways submit to him, and he will make your paths straight.
—Proverbs 3:5-6, NIV

We are to trust the Lord at all times. During the day and at night. We can't possibly lean on our understanding because we cannot know all things. Even the most brilliant people on Earth can't explain all things. God gave us complex minds, but they are finite. We have limits, but the Lord is limitless.

As we hear God's Word, we must put our faith into action and believe what He says. Even when we have questions concerning our futures. How is it possible that what God has in store for us is any better than what He took? Where is our assurance that saying *yes* to an unseen plan will fulfill us as our dreams once did? And will we achieve anything as noteworthy as we did when living our dreams? The answer to all these questions is Isaiah 55:8-9. God's thoughts are not our thoughts, and His ways are not our ways. As the heavens are higher than the Earth, so are His ways higher than ours and His thoughts higher than our thoughts. This is why we must trust Him with our uncertainty.

Imagine that what you hoped to achieve while living your dream does not compare to the fruit you will bear following Christ.

"No eye has seen, no ear has heard, and no mind has imagined what God has prepared for those who love him."
—1 Corinthians 2:9, NLT

And the Lord teaches us that loving Him is to obey Him.

Jesus answered him, "If anyone loves me, he will keep my word, and my Father will love him, and we will come to him and make our home with him."
—John 14:23, ESV

Obeying Christ's calling to leave your dream means that you truly love Him. Those that love Him are His true disciples. We may not be able to imagine a meaningful life down an unseen pathway, but God tells us in His

Word that we also cannot imagine what He has planned for us who love Him. Ponder that truth for a moment.

There was a time when Josh wanted to return to what he loved. He tried to return to the tangible and meaningful game because baseball meant more than pursuing the unknown. He made phone calls and even continued working out, keeping his physical frame in shape just in case the opportunity arose for him to have another shot. But deep down, he knew that he wasn't supposed to pursue his past. Waiting on the unknown to reveal itself was torturous for Josh because sitting still was difficult for him to do. In the Old Testament, the Israelites acted in a very similar way.

When Moses went to Egypt to deliver the Israelites and lead them to a land promised to them, the people had been slaves for over 400 years. Think about that. These people were literal slaves in Egypt, and one day a man showed up to free them. If you were one of them, would you have trusted the one who wanted to unshackle you? Would you have packed your things up and left, or would the fear of an unknown future keep you in bondage?

This massive exodus was successful after a series of plagues God poured out on the Egyptians. It was so bad that the Egyptians themselves told the people to leave for fear that all the Egyptians would die (Exodus 12:33). The road ahead of the Israelites wasn't easy. They had to cross a sea, depend on God for food in the desert, and trust that their sandals wouldn't wear out. And God took care of them despite their grumblings. But at one point, the people started to turn back because their pasts outshined the difficulty of what lay ahead. God told their forefathers many years prior that they would occupy a promised area of land. This land, however, had other people inhabiting it. So instead of trusting the Lord, the people grew frustrated and began complaining to Moses and his brother Aaron.

"If only we had died in Egypt! Or in this wilderness! Why is the Lord bringing us to this land only to let us fall by the sword? Our wives and children will be taken as plunder. Wouldn't it be better for us to go back to Egypt?" And they said to each other, "We should choose a leader and go back to Egypt."

—Numbers 14:2-4, NIV

Fear caused the men to desire their past, a place of slavery, because their future was frightening. But God already promised their future.

Since when is slavery more appealing than freedom? When our paths require us to depend entirely on God because, in those moments, we become vulnerable. And most do not like the feeling of vulnerability. I would argue that the Israelites were not advocating for slavery but a place of normalcy. A place where they understood life. Not that life as slaves far surpassed their dreams, but it was one where everything had its place. The people knew where to work, how to find and prepare food, and they sensed protection no matter how frugal it was. They could not perceive that the benefits of moving forward with the Lord outweighed the notion to turn back.

Thankfully two men, Joshua and Caleb, who had explored the promised land, stood in front of the Israelites and spoke these words:

> *"The land we passed through and explored is exceedingly good. If the Lord is pleased with us, he will lead us into that land, a land flowing with milk and honey, and will give it to us. Only do not rebel against the Lord. And do not be afraid of the people of the land, because we will devour them. Their protection is gone, but the Lord is with us. Do not be afraid of them."*
>
> **—Numbers 14:7-9, NIV**

And what does the Lord say to us? The same words. *Do not be afraid.* If God is for us, who could be against us? (Romans 8:31). What could have been in your life doesn't matter when the Spirit teaches us to strain towards what is ahead, forgetting what is behind (Philippians 3:13).

I encourage you to step forward no matter how foolish your direction appears to onlookers. You are not following Christ to appease others; you are doing so out of your love for the One who died for you.

What you never accomplished while living your dream doesn't compare to what you are yet to achieve while following Him. Allow the Lord to reveal what you cannot see.

A Prayer for Your Journey:

Lord, though I cannot see where you are leading me, I trust you alone know the way. Help me to stay committed to the path in front of me. Be my vision Lord when I cannot see what you are doing. In Jesus' name, I pray, Amen.

A Hymn to Ponder:

Be Thou My Vision[5]

Written By: Eleanor Hull
Song By: Elenyi

Be thou my vision, O Lord of my heart
Naught be all else to me, save that thou art
Thou my best thought, by day or by night
Waking or sleeping, thy presence my light

Be thou my wisdom, and thou my true word
I ever with thee and thou with me, Lord
Thou my great Father, and I thy true son
Thou in me dwelling and I with thee one

Riches I heed not, nor man's empty praise
Thou mine inheritance, now and always
Thou and thou only first in my heart
High King of heaven, my treasure thou art

High King of heaven, my victory won
May I reach heaven's joys, O bright heaven's sun
Heart of my own heart, whatever befall
Still be my vision, O ruler of all

Be thou my vision

---

[5] "Be Thou My Vision - ELENYI Version (with Lyrics Cc) - on SPOTIFY & Apple Music." 2017. www.youtube.com. December 15, 2017. https://www.youtube.com/watch?v=_VpSqAcLrDI.

Chapter 5

Let's Go to the Other Side

When I read about Jesus' disciples in the Bible, I am continually amazed at what they could see and do. They were ordinary people like you and me, yet they walked with Christ witnessing miracles of all kinds. Sometimes we put them on pedestals imagining them being better Christians than the rest of us. But that's not so. Wrapped in the flesh, they struggled with many of the same trials that we face today. Yet, despite their shortcomings, God chose them to follow Him, and they did.

One place they followed Christ was onto a boat.

One day Jesus said to his disciples, "Let us go over to the other side of the lake." So they got into a boat and set out.
—Luke 8:22, NIV

First, we must recognize that Jesus said, "let us," meaning He was with them on this venture. Then, as we continue reading, we notice that the disciples willingly followed Him. Scripture doesn't say that they feared storms, for several were fishermen. But this trip certainly included one. Notice what Jesus does as soon as He gets inside the boat:

As they sailed, he fell asleep.
—Luke 8:23, NIV

I've often laughed at this scripture mainly because I imagine the type of boat they must have boarded. This vessel wasn't a cruise ship with lovely cabins. I'm reasonably sure that Jesus didn't have any Dramamine on deck in case He or His disciples felt nauseated. And while Jesus slept, all was well. What a peaceful scene it must have been on that boat with the Savior of the world. I'm sure the disciples felt that if Jesus were calm enough to sleep, no harm would come to them. But this assurance was brief:

And a windstorm came down on the lake, and they were filling with water and were in danger.
—Luke 8:23, ESV

This storm must have caught the disciples by surprise because, after all, Jesus was sleeping. The boat was filling with water—what a terrifying experience. The disciples did what you and I probably would have done:

The disciples went and woke him, saying, "Master, Master, we're going to drown!"
—Luke 8:24, NIV

They didn't approach Jesus casually; they came to Him out of fear. In other words, they implied that if Jesus didn't get up, they would all die. And what was His response?

He got up and rebuked the wind and the raging waters; the storm subsided, and all was calm. "Where is your faith?" he asked his disciples.
—Luke 8:24-25, NIV

Jesus spoke to the storm before speaking to His followers. Once the storm relented, everything was at ease. Christ then turned towards the disciples and asked an earnest question. Where was their faith? It took Jesus calming the storm before the disciples could calm down. Can you relate to this? I know I can. Humans have so many emotions that it's challenging to be still and trust the Lord when our boats are filling with water. Until the situation changes, it's almost natural to panic.

But having faith means believing what God tells us. How quickly the disciples forgot His words.

Going back to Luke 8:22, He told the disciples, *"Let us go over to the other side of the lake."* He never said, "Let us go over to the other side of the lake if we can or if there isn't a storm." Christ's words teach us that being with

Him doesn't mean we will not encounter trials. We most certainly will, because He tells us upfront that we will have trouble (John 16:33). And if Jesus says that we're going to the other side, we will arrive no matter what happens in the process.

This story also teaches us that Jesus will see us through anything we face. It may appear as though He is sleeping when we are in our most desperate hour; but remember what He says in His Word:

I will never leave you nor forsake you.
—Joshua 1:5, NIV

For a very long time, I thought I had climbed into the boat, metaphorically, to follow Christ alongside my husband. We've experienced our fair share of trials, including the loss of Josh's dream. For years the storms raged, and I prayed fervently for my husband's joy to return. As I write these words, it wasn't until now that I realized I'm on the boat for other reasons. I'm not only occupying a seat in support of my husband, but I'm also here to share a trial of my own.

On November 1, 2021, I received a phone call from my doctor that changed the course of my life. She told me that I had breast cancer. As the words entered my ears, I had difficulty processing what she said. It was an ordinary weekday evening when I dropped my son off at basketball practice. After she said that I had cancer, my vehicle came to a stop in front of the middle school gym. My son said he loved me as he opened the door to get out, and I sat there silent. Of course, I didn't tell him the news.

How could a 38-year-old have breast cancer without any immediate or extended family history of the disease? I thought I was a pretty healthy person. In those moments, water started filling my boat. Instead of crying out to God, I just started crying. No, I began sobbing. Then I called my mom. I could barely speak as my throat clenched and tears flowed down my face.

My mom has been a nurse for over 40 years, and I knew she would know what to do. I'm what she calls "medically illiterate," meaning that I don't pay attention to anything medical. She and my stepdad, who is also a nurse, still laugh at the story of me giving a science lesson to a group of kindergartners during my first year of teaching. The students had an outline of the human body and a few parts to attach. One such part was the trachea. Staring at the image, I had no idea what it was or where to put it. I ever so slightly turned my back to the class as they were working so I could get a better look at the image and decided that it probably would go on the neck. So, I turned back around and enthusiastically told the class that this unique part helps us talk. I asked them where they thought we should glue it, and of course, they said the mouth. I told them they were close. And, unbeknownst to me at the time, I glued my trachea on upside down. Thank the Lord my pupils weren't much older than five years old.

Truly my mom can laugh all she wants because I still bug her about having to take a Tylenol for nearly every ailment I had growing up. Yes, I had four other siblings fighting for her attention, but I think my arm could have fallen off, and she would have told me to take a Tylenol. So, because of my carefree way of looking at medical issues, I never once thought the lump I found a few months prior was cancerous. Instead, I thought I had pulled a muscle pushing a hefty filing cabinet across my office at work. When I told my mom my assumptions, her voice shifted to an "are you kidding me?" tone and carefully explained that people do not get lumps in their breasts from pushing filing cabinets. Hmm, I guess she was right.

After the initial conversation with my mom, I knew I had to talk to Josh. I didn't want to do it over the phone, so I waited until we were both at home. As much as I desired to tell him, I also dreaded it. I had never really been sick. Certainly not with a sickness that would change our family's day-to-day life and, what I most feared, the way Josh would see me. This year marks nineteen years of marriage, and I still look at him like I did in high school. I didn't want his view to be any different.

When the garage door opened, I waited for him to walk through the door. When he and my son rounded the corner, I spoke through my shaky voice and told them I needed to talk to them. Struggling to get the words out, I finally managed to say that I had breast cancer. Josh's head hung down as the room became eerily silent. He knew that I had a mass on my right side, but I think I had almost convinced him that it was nothing. I told him so many times before not to worry about it, and now here I was, standing in the middle of the house with tears running down my face.

Because it *was* something. It was something that blindsided us.

I had built a relationship with the Lord, and honestly never thought something like this would happen. Like me, you may pray daily for God's protection over your family. And so, it's difficult to explain the feeling of receiving life-threatening news. I'm sure the disciples never dreamed they would endure a storm either, but they did. Now I was experiencing one. Scary news like this can choke our faith when our emotions shatter.

Josh and I didn't know what to expect or what the road ahead looked like, because all we felt in those moments was darkness. The water was rising, and the storm began raging. Was God asleep?

After a brief period, Josh came towards me and put his arms around me. He said that everything was going to be okay. As much as I needed his assurance, my gaze drifted towards my son. He didn't look panicked at all. It must have been my "you'll be fine" kind of parenting, because he looked at me as I was wiping my face and asked if I was going to be okay. I told him I was. He shrugged his shoulders and said, "Okay," and walked towards his room. He wasn't dazed in the least. He took me for my word. I said I was going to be okay, and he believed me. So did my daughter when I told her later, but she was worried about another issue--me losing my hair.

My body was going to change, and I knew it. I stood in front of my bathroom mirror and imagined every strand of hair falling out. And I have a lot of hair! But God tells us in His Word that even the very hairs of our heads are all numbered (Matthew 10:30), so I said to Him that His job was about to get a whole lot easier. Then I started crying again.

Dying to ourselves isn't easy, but Jesus requires this before following Him.

A wealthy young man in the book of Matthew illustrates this hardship. After asking Jesus what he must do to get eternal life, Christ tells him to obey the Commandments. The man then tells the Lord that he has kept all the Commandments and asks what he still lacks. Jesus' response pinpoints what the rich man had a tight grip on.

Jesus answered, "If you want to be perfect, go, sell your possessions and give to the poor, and you will have treasure in heaven. Then come, follow me."

—Matthew 19:21, NIV

Was Jesus asking too much of the young man? Is He asking too much from you or me? No. He knew what prevented the man from dying to himself. The Lord also knows what prevents us from drawing closer and going deeper with Him. It's possible for us to have a relationship with God, yet still lack something that keeps us from moving forward with Him.

The person in the story had built a life on Earth as one intent on staying, not passing through. To follow Christ, we must be willing to deny ourselves and pick up our cross daily (Luke 9:23). How did the man in the story react to Jesus' words?

When the young man heard this, he went away sad, because he had great wealth.
—Matthew 19:22, NIV

To surrender earthly wealth was too high a price for the man to pay. But what good is it for someone to gain the world yet forfeit his soul? (Matthew 16:26). One of the most challenging acts for us is to live in the world but not be of it. Wealth isn't the only thing preventing some of us from following Christ wholeheartedly. What about our relationships? Our priorities? Our secrets? What if dying to ourselves requires cancer treatments and hair loss? Storms come in many forms, but they stretch our faith because faith without action is dead (James 2:26).

Getting into Christ's boat requires commitment but following Him costs us everything. Unfortunately, we often look for the reward of our commitment without first considering the cost. A mother did this in the book of Matthew. Listen to what she asked Jesus regarding her two sons:

Then the mother of Zebedee's sons came to Jesus with her sons and, kneeling down, asked a favor of him.
"What is it you want?" he asked.
She said, "Grant that one of these two sons of mine may sit at your right and the other at your left in your kingdom."
"You don't know what you are asking," Jesus said to them. "Can you drink the cup I am going to drink?"
"We can," they answered.
Jesus said to them, "You will indeed drink from my cup, but to sit at my right or left is not for me to grant. These places belong to those for whom they have been prepared by my Father."
—Matthew 20:20-23, NIV

This mom probably believed that since her sons were committed to Christ, her request wasn't unreasonable. Jesus quickly points out to the mom that it was. He then turns to the sons who have accompanied her and asks them if they can drink the same cup as Him. What's impressive is that they immediately say that they could. Clearly, they did not understand the magnitude of what the Savior was asking. Is it possible for any of us to drink the same cup as Christ? There isn't one person on the planet, past or present, that can identify with bearing the entire world's sins to save the lost.

But Jesus tells the sons *yes*, they will indeed drink from His cup. In other words, they will share in His sufferings, but sitting at His right or left isn't for Him to grant. Take hold of this truth: drinking from Christ's cup requires us to pour ourselves out *so that we can* share in His sufferings (Matthew 26:27-28) and also share in His glory (Romans 8:16-17).

Dying to ourselves is a painful process. Until the Lord leads us into a storm, however, many of us will never experience a pouring out.

When Josh lost his dream, he told me that he didn't know he had any pride in him to get rid of. I didn't recognize it either. I always viewed Josh as one of the humblest people I'd ever met. But the Lord required Josh to pour himself out before following Him. Yes, he was a Christian, but he hadn't surrendered every area of his life. That process was emotionally painful. It was confusing for him to understand at the time, and it was far more confusing to explain by the world's measures. The world paints a picture of failure when someone's career doesn't last. This experience causes grave disappointment if that's where our hope lies.

Suffering, however, produces perseverance. Perseverance produces character. Character produces hope. And hope does not disappoint us! (Romans 5:3-5). Look at the process one must experience before having a hope that doesn't disappoint.

Can you identify with people who say they never get their "hopes up" because they do not want to feel disappointed? The Bible teaches us the contrary. There isn't any disappointment found in hope when it's rooted in the Lord (Isaiah 49:23). If you find yourself dissatisfied, you most likely feel let down because a situation didn't turn out the way you wanted. But going back to suffering, when we share in Christ's sufferings, the experience creates perseverance. Despite the difficulties we face, the Lord enables us to continue in our course of action. And pressing forward develops our character or the backbone of our individuality. Someone once told me that character is who we are when no one is looking. There is a lot of truth to this statement. Such character produces hope. Therefore, we can expect God to do what He says He will, not what we expect to gain by our means.

Anything we anticipate achieving by our means is a false hope. And false hope always disappoints. God does not disappoint us; it's our reactions to the storms we face that let us down. We often panic or fall to pieces when we are supposed to remember what He tells us.

One morning in October 2021, I was reading the Word when God spoke Matthew 9:22 to me. He told me that my faith had healed me. I didn't know exactly what He was referring to at that moment, but when I received the news of cancer on November 1, I later remembered what He said:

Jesus turned and saw her. "Take heart, daughter," he said, "your faith has healed you." And the woman was healed at that moment.
—Matthew 9:22, NIV

I then had a choice to make. Was I going to believe God or not? From the moment God spoke His Word to me, He healed me. He told me He healed me from cancer before I even knew I had the disease. And He told the disciples they were going to the other side of the lake before they encountered the storm. The situations are no different. Are we going to believe what God tells us?

We must believe God's Word because our faith brings healing. The disappointment, then, can come from how God fulfills His Word. We're let down if it's not how we want it to be.

After remembering what God told me, I shared the excitement with Josh. Together, we knew that God was healing my body. Not that we didn't have days that were sad or a struggle to get through, but we clung to what the Lord said because God cannot lie (Titus 1:2).

I told the Lord that I knew He could heal me instantly. I could walk into my next doctor's appointment, and the scans could indicate no cancer! God can do that. Indeed, my family, friends, pastor, and church were all praying for this. I believed that if complete instant healing was His will, then that's what would happen.

But deep down, I knew God was leading me through the storm, not around it.

On November 12, 2021, the Lord told me to drink from His cup. He said He healed me, but that I would receive treatment for cancer. After suffering for a little while, He will raise me up (1 Peter 5:6). This treatment meant all of it: chemotherapy, radiation, and surgery. I would feel sick and lose my hair. I wasn't going to die from cancer, but I would certainly die to myself. That's a difficult drink to swallow. But it's required of me to follow Christ where He is taking me.

What is God requiring of you? Is He guiding you through a storm that you don't want to face? Ask Him to help you as He takes you across deep waters.

Josh believed me when I shared God's Word with him, but the truth also bothered him. My husband didn't want me to endure one second of treatment. But, again, our wants can let us down, and they can cause us to be disappointed in Christ. We feel dismayed because we know God can spare us of anything. When He chooses a different means to get us to the other side of a storm, we tend to withdraw from Him when we should be clinging to His Word.

Consider that sometimes God leaves us in a place to change our own lives. Then at other times, God moves us to change the lives of others.

King Solomon teaches us about seasons of life in the book of Ecclesiastes. He points out that there is a time for everything under heaven.

a time to be born and a time to die,
a time to plant and a time to uproot,
a time to kill and a time to heal,
a time to tear down and a time to build,
a time to weep and a time to laugh,
a time to mourn and a time to dance,
a time to scatter stones and a time to gather them,
a time to embrace and a time to refrain from embracing,
a time to search and a time to give up,
a time to keep and a time to throw away,
a time to tear and a time to mend,
a time to be silent and a time to speak,
a time to love and a time to hate,
a time for war and a time for peace.
What do workers gain from their toil? I have seen the burden God has laid on the human race. He has made everything beautiful in its time.
—Ecclesiastes 3:2-11, NIV

In time, God makes everything beautiful. Even physical beauty that is lost. Though following Him may cost us our dreams, we will never be disappointed for having lost something for the sake of His kingdom.

God is leading me, and perhaps you, through a storm and not around it because we are moving forward with Him. And sometimes, moving forward includes suffering. So, in our moments of suffering, let us throw off everything that hinders us and take hold of the hope we profess. For He who is leading us is faithful (Hebrews 10:23).

When we have a relationship with Christ and move forward with Him to accomplish His will, we learn more of His nature, and trusting Him becomes easier. After Jesus rebuked the winds and the raging waters for His disciples, the Bible says that all was calm (Luke 8:24). But if we read further, we discover a bizarre reaction from the disciples:

In fear and amazement they asked one another, "Who is this? He commands even the winds and the water, and they obey him."
—Luke 8:25, NIV

Why on Earth would the disciples still ask who Jesus was after all they had experienced with Him? They physically saw what many of us only read about in scripture. Even after witnessing the wind and the waves obey Jesus, they still questioned who He was. Yet, in the chapters leading up to the storm, Luke notes the following experiences the disciples had with the Savior.

- Along with James and John, Peter witnessed a miraculous catch of fish that Jesus provided them, because they simply obeyed His command to put out into deep water and let down their nets (Luke 5:1-11).
- They witnessed Jesus heal a man with leprosy and a person with paralysis

  (Luke 5:12-26).
- They witnessed Jesus heal a man with a shriveled hand (Luke 6:1-11).
- They witnessed Jesus heal people of many different diseases and cure those troubled by evil spirits (Luke 6:18).

- They witnessed Jesus teach to large crowds about loving their enemies and not judging others (Luke 6:27-42).
- They witnessed the faith of a centurion and the healing of his servant (Luke 7:1-10).
- They witnessed Jesus raise a dead son back to life and return him to his mother (Luke 7:11-17).
- They witnessed a sinful woman anointing Jesus and Him forgiving her of her sins (Luke 7:36-50).
- They traveled with Jesus and saw Him proclaim the good news of the kingdom of God to many people (Luke 8:1).

All these encounters occurred before the storm. So, it's no wonder Jesus asked them, *"Where is your faith?"* (Luke 8:25, NIV). They struggled to comprehend Jesus as Lord and Savior. But even if they couldn't wrap their minds around Jesus Himself, at least they could have believed in the miracles themselves (John 14:11). Later, we learn in Luke Chapter 19 that the disciples did begin praising the Lord for all they had witnessed and experienced, but it took time for them to arrive at such a place.

What about us and our experiences with God? Have we spent enough time with Him to marvel at His power? If we are amidst a storm, can we rest as He did as the waters fill our boats and the winds toss us about? We can most assuredly rest in our storm by remembering what the Lord has told us and believing what He's said.

You have climbed into the boat with Christ, and He has told you that you will go to the other side. So, trust His words and allow Him to lead you through unchartered waters to a deeper relationship with Him.

A Prayer for Your Journey:

Lord, help me to recount my experiences with you. You have told me that we are going to the other side of my trial. I trust that together we will get there. In Jesus' name, I pray, Amen.

A Hymn to Ponder:

Wonderful, Merciful Savior[6]

Written By: Selah

Wonderful, merciful Savior
Precious Redeemer and Friend
Who would've thought that a Lamb could
Rescue the souls of men
Oh, You rescue the souls of men

Counselor, Comforter, Keeper
Spirit we long to embrace
You offer hope when our hearts have
Hopelessly lost our way
Oh, we've hopelessly lost the way

You are the One that we praise
You are the One we adore
You give the healing and grace
Our hearts always hunger for
Oh, our hearts always hunger for

Almighty, infinite Father
Faithfully loving Your own
Here in our weakness You find us
Falling before Your throne
Oh, we're falling before Your throne

You are the One that we praise
You are the One we adore
You give the healing and grace
Our hearts always hunger for
Oh, our hearts always hunger for

---

6 "Selah - 'Wonderful Merciful Savior' (Official Video)." 2016. www.youtube.com. August 22, 2016. https://www.youtube.com/watch?v=fK6sYVQCqhs.

You are the One that we praise
You are the One we adore
You give the healing and grace
Our hearts always hunger for
Oh, our hearts always hunger for

Chapter 6

Unshackled

Emerging from a storm is prevented when we are shackled or bound. Many hindrances in life lurk around us and some tie us down, keeping us from ever experiencing the freedom in Christ He so desires for us to have. A pastor friend of mine, one I consider a faithful prayer warrior, encouraged me to read the book *Two Hours to Freedom*. The author, Charles H. Kraft, states something most spectacular in his writing: Christians can be saved but not free[7].

It's a statement that must roll around in your mind a few times before it finds a resting place to sink in. But after chewing on the words for a bit, we can better understand the meaning. Christians can actually live their lives without ever experiencing freedom. Theoretically, this doesn't make much sense, because when people accept Christ as their Savior, the Holy Spirit comes to dwell within their soul. Isn't that freedom enough? Yes, salvation allows us to spend eternity with the Lord, but it doesn't necessarily give freedom on Earth. More is required of us.

In the book of John, Jesus begins speaking to a group of Jews about what freedom in Him means. But first, notice how Jesus describes them:

---

[7] Kraft, Charles H. 2010. *Two Hours to Freedom: A Simple and Effective Model for Healing and Deliverance*. Grand Rapids, Mich.: Chosen Books.

To the Jews who had believed him, Jesus said,
—John 8:31, NIV

Jesus makes it clear in this scripture that the group of people He is speaking to initially believed His words. This means they placed their faith in what Christ said. Reading on, however, we discover that they didn't easily understand Jesus' definition of freedom:

"If you hold to my teaching, you are really my disciples. Then you will know the truth, and the truth will set you free."
—John 8:31-32, NIV

So, the only way to know the truth is to hold to Jesus' teaching, and this truth will set us free. Keeping Jesus' teaching means we believe and obey His words. Now, the group of Jews that Jesus was having this conversation with didn't quite understand what Jesus was saying. They told the Lord that they were Abraham's descendants and had never been a slave to anyone. In their minds, they were already free. But we know Jesus wasn't referring to physical chains:

Jesus replied, "Very truly I tell you, everyone who sins is a slave to sin. Now a slave has no permanent place in the family, but a son belongs to it forever. So if the Son sets you free, you will be free indeed. I know that you are Abraham's descendants. Yet you are looking for a way to kill me, because you have no room for my word. I am telling you what I have seen in the Father's presence, and you are doing what you have heard from your father."
—John 8:34-38, NIV

The people may have believed Jesus, but they had no room for His Word. Having room requires space, and for most of us to free up space, we must first get rid of clutter. Therefore, we must choose between who we're going to obey, because we cannot follow God *and* Satan. The group Jesus spoke to had no space to obey the Word of God, and that's why Jesus told them that they do what they have heard from *their* father--not God the Father.

Again, we can believe Jesus but live as slaves because we have no room to obey His teachings. A slave to obedience leads to righteousness, and a slave to sin leads to death (Romans 6:16). We are a slave to the one we obey.

Thank God! Once you were slaves of sin, but now you wholeheartedly obey this teaching we have given you. Now you are free from your slavery to sin, and you have become slaves to righteous living.

—Romans 6:17-18, NLT

God trusts us with His Word. He wants us to honor it and live it, because that space sets captives free.

As we follow the Lord wholeheartedly, He gives us spiritual freedom because in Him we live, move, and have our being (Acts 17:28). Those who have lost their dream for the sake of following Christ know the immense heartache that comes with such a loss. But that decision alone, to leave what we love in this life, shows our faithfulness.

If we are not carrying out Christ's desires for our lives, we carry out the devil's. Consider how Jesus describes the enemy in the following scripture.

He was a murderer from the beginning, not holding to the truth, for there is no truth in him. When he lies, he speaks his native language, for he is a liar and the father of lies.

—John 8:44, NIV

Satan has been a murderer *from the beginning,* and he didn't *hold to the truth.* Therefore, he isn't free. And freedom is something he never wants us to experience.

We must hold to Christ's teachings for the truth to be in us. If not, then we speak lies. That's exactly what Satan does. He speaks lies, and he wants us to do the same. On that path, we'll never become Christ's disciples. So, is it possible for us to read the Word and believe it but not remain faithful to it? Yes, it's possible. That's how we stay slaves to sin.

Believers have a way to resist the sinful nature, or not be controlled by it, and that is through the Holy Spirit. But if we do not grow in our faith, we will not have the strength to resist such sin.

For years after baseball ended, Josh merely existed rather than lived. He did look for comfort when he opened his Bible, but he wasn't seeking Christ to live, he was seeking comfort to exist. This scenario may not sound that frightening, but if Jesus says that holding to His Word reveals truth and the truth sets us free, then Josh wasn't free because he wasn't receiving the whole truth. Likewise, if we only choose to read certain scriptures, then we are bound because we miss out on the fullness of Christ.

Deep hurts can cause restlessness and keep us out of the Word entirely. We may recall scriptures we learned from childhood but remaining out of the Word means we are not continuing in it. To continue in something means to practice it. The behavior requires intentionality. Thinking about reading the Bible is not the same thing as reading it.

For an extended period, Josh did a whole lot of thinking rather than doing, without realizing the consequences of such complacency. As a result, his thoughts drifted, his actions grew negative, and his spiritual life suffered. He became a slave to disappointing thoughts that lingered. Initially, this subtle habit kept him from moving forward. He temporarily had eyes but couldn't see and ears but couldn't hear (Psalm 115:5-6).

Not providing space for what God is doing can cause hostility towards His plan. This resistance can be physical, as is seen in John 8. But it can also be a negative disposition or refusal to follow. Our thoughts alone can prevent us from obeying God's Word, and this is why the Lord teaches us to hold our thoughts captive (2 Corinthians 10:5). We must cage our ideas and make them obedient to God, because we're born with a sinful desire to do the opposite.

When God calls us to something different in life, we must put into practice the action of holding our thoughts captive. If not, we're in danger of our thoughts holding *us* captive. That's when darkness sneaks in, and the enemy does his best to confuse us.

Lance Berkman, Josh's former teammate with the Houston Astros, said in an interview in May 2021 that leaving the game of baseball was like experiencing a death[8]. This experience caused him to question who he was after his dream ended. And yet, this interview was announcing Berkman's new position as the Head Baseball Coach for Houston Baptist University. A chance for him to have a second career.

Can you relate to second choices not replacing the fulfillment you received from your initial dream?

Another athlete, boxing legend Sugar Ray Leonard, said that outside the ring nothing could satisfy him. Magnifying this feeling, he said that

---

8 "HBU Announcement: Lance Berkman as Head Baseball Coach." 2021. www.youtube.com. May 31, 2021. https://www.youtube.com/watch?v=qxLRaujf7Ck.

nothing in life could compare to becoming a world champion, with his hand raised, and millions of people cheering him on[9].

Why is it so difficult to move on from a previous dream? It could be that when we are on the receiving end of glory, willingly giving up praise is deflating.

I believe anyone who has the opportunity to live their dreams is fulfilled not only because they are able to use their talents, but because other people see them and appreciate them. When the dreams die, the same loyal fans who praised such gifts may easily forget they ever existed.

And if we do not continue in God's Word, like once loyal fans, we can easily forget what the Lord has told us. Deteriorating thoughts can bind us to the point of becoming slaves to them.

Do you believe what God has told you in your relationship with Him? And are you holding on or remaining faithful to His Word? If so, God's truth has set you free. If not, this is a good time to remember what He's said. Christ knows your hurts, heartbreaks, and fears. He also understands the impact of His Word to you.

"Blessed is anyone who does not stumble on account of me."
—Luke 7:23, NIV

Following Jesus requires us to make difficult decisions--ones that affect our families and careers. The Lord is fully aware of this and doesn't want any one of us to fall away on account of what He's doing in our lives.

One way to stay connected to God's Word and remember His promises is to record dates in your Bible beside scriptures He speaks to you. I started doing this in 2007. The first date I wrote down was next to this verse:

"I have heard your prayer and seen your tears; I will heal you."
—2 Kings 20:5, NIV

At the time, I was praying to become a mom. I didn't know if I would get to hold a baby of my own in my arms because my husband and I had

---

[9] Vickers, Emma. 2015. "Sports Psychology – Depression in the Retired Athlete." The UK's Leading Sports Psychology Website. March 30, 2015. https://believeperform.com/life-after-sport-depression-in-retired-athletes/.

tried with no success. I couldn't help but think there was something wrong with me physically, so I prayed and asked God to heal me.

And He did.

Two more years passed, and I had a miscarriage before that scripture came to pass. But it happened, and I'll never forget God's words to me. Fast-forward fourteen years, and this time God spoke the answer to a prayer I hadn't yet prayed. He told me my faith healed me before knowing I had breast cancer. This is what a love relationship with the Savior of the world is like.

Dates recorded in your Bible will remind you daily of who you are in Christ. You will never forget His words to you as you turn the pages. And these words will loosen your shackles and allow you to hold your thoughts captive, making them obedient to a God who first loved you.

When Dreams Lost Look Different

For some of us, dreams lost look differently than previously described. We haven't all experienced losing a career, but some have experienced dreams lost through the destructive actions of others. The Lord recently reminded me that I have experienced this and need to share the following words with you.

As a young girl, I used to look at other families and wonder what it would be like to have a loving, earthly father in my life. Unfortunately, my dream of having such a relationship shattered early on. When I was seven, my parents divorced due to my father's alcoholism and violent behavior.

Though my siblings and I were still in my father's life for some time after the separation, his abusive actions didn't subside. Sadly, I was on the receiving end of his abuse.

There was nothing more confusing than hearing Jesus loved me on Sunday and then later being abused by someone else who also said he loved me. If Jesus loved me, then why didn't He prevent my hurt? Have you ever asked that question? If you can't identify with an abusive relationship, perhaps you can with a torn marriage or a strained parental connection. When others have hurt us, the enemy wants us to believe a gospel contrary to the truth we initially received.

To deceive us, the enemy persuades us to believe that if God truly loved us, He would have prevented us from ever experiencing pain. And because God didn't stop this, Satan encourages us to blame the Lord. In Galatians, Paul warns us not to believe such perversion of the truth:

I am astonished that you are so quickly deserting the one who called you to live in the grace of Christ and are turning to a different gospel – which is really no gospel at all. Evidently some people are throwing you into confusion and are trying to pervert the gospel of Christ.

—Galatians 1:6-7, NIV

The one who will always distort the gospel of Christ is Satan himself. So, let's first cast the blame on him. Our God is not a God of confusion but peace (1 Corinthians 14:33). And our fight is not against flesh and blood but the spiritual forces of evil (Ephesians 6:12).

Recentering, then, where is the Lord when we experience trials or are on the receiving end of others' violent acts? He is with us. In the book of Daniel, God gives us a picture of this truth:

Then King Nebuchadnezzar leaped to his feet in amazement and asked his advisors, "Weren't there three men that we tied up and threw into the fire?"
They replied, "Certainly, Your Majesty."
He said, "Look! I see four men walking around in the fire, unbound and unharmed, and the fourth looks like a son of the gods."

—Daniel 3:24-25, NIV

God allowed King Nebuchadnezzar to see Himself alongside His followers as the fate of their lives hung in the balance. The three men thrown into the blazing fire for not renouncing their faith still experienced the trial--but came out unscathed. The men believed in God's ability to save and restore them over Satan's lie that God wouldn't. This belief rescued them.

And when someone has wronged us, our freedom begins with forgiveness.

Astonishingly, one in four practicing Christians (around 23%) can identify one person who they "just can't forgive."[10] But we cannot heal from past hurts unless we dissolve feelings of anger or resentment. There is power in forgiving someone who has wronged us or in asking for

---

[10] "1 in 4 Practicing Christians Struggles to Forgive Someone." 2019. Barna Group. 2019. https://www.barna.com/research/forgiveness-christians/.

forgiveness from someone we have afflicted. This action provides us freedom, allowing Christ to forgive us for the sins we have committed. Jesus tells us that if we don't forgive, He Himself will not forgive us (Matthew 6:15). And if Christ doesn't forgive us, we are bound and lost forever.

When I was thirty-one years old, the Lord arranged an opportunity for me to verbally tell my dad something I had internally done many years prior. As my aunt prepared to transition into a new home, I offered to help her with the move. When I walked into her house, I was unaware that my dad was there. As we packed up my aunt's belongings, she wanted us to stop at my dad's house before making the rest of the trip to give him some things she didn't plan to take with her. When we finished unloading the items, I turned around to head towards my vehicle. My aunt had already left, so I was in haste to get going as well. But something stopped me as I was walking towards my car.

My dad called me by my name.

I couldn't remember the last time I heard him do that. When I heard my name, I turned towards him. It was just like Mary Magdalene when Jesus called her by name, and she turned towards Him (John 20:16). Mary gave her Heavenly Father space to speak, and I gave my earthly father that same space.

Then, from his front porch, the words "I'm sorry" fell from my dad's lips. I couldn't believe what I was hearing. He said he was sorry for what he did to me, my mom, and my siblings. When he finished, it took me a minute to respond. Finally, with a shaky voice I told him that I had already forgiven him. It wasn't a long conversation but one that needed to happen. Before turning to my car, I told him I loved him and then left.

Driving away, I looked in my rearview mirror and saw him watch me leave. Then, as tears ran down my face, I felt chains fall from my wrists and ankles. Forgiving my dad didn't change what he did, but it set me free.

You can receive this same freedom.

Seeking Forgiveness from the World, rather than Christ

One of Jesus' twelve disciples made the mistake of not seeking Christ for forgiveness. He turned to the world instead of the only One who could have saved him. His name is Judas Iscariot. Let's read about what he did in the book of Luke:

Now the Feast of Unleavened Bread, called the Passover, was approaching, and the chief priests and the teachers of the law were looking for some way to get rid of Jesus, for they were afraid of the people. Then Satan entered Judas, called Iscariot, one of the Twelve. And Judas went to the chief priests and the officers of the temple guard and discussed with them how he might betray Jesus. They were delighted and agreed to give him money. He consented, and watched for an opportunity to hand Jesus over to them when no crowd was present.

—Luke 22:1-6, NIV

It's hard for us to fathom one of the twelve disciples betraying Jesus. Based solely on the miracles Judas Iscariot witnessed, how could he willingly decide to betray his Savior? Verse 6 of Luke 20 has two words that answer this: *He consented.* To consent to something means to give permission. Judas gave Satan permission to enter him. Growing up, I heard many people say, "Poor Judas never had a prayer. God had to choose someone to betray Him, so He chose Judas." I beg to differ. Yes, God is all-knowing, and He knew who would betray Him, but Judas had free will just as we do.

Judas chose to obey Satan rather than God and was later remorseful for what he did.

Early in the morning, all the chief priests and the elders of the people made their plans how to have Jesus executed. So they bound him, led him away and handed him over to Pilate the governor. When Judas, who had betrayed him, saw that Jesus was condemned, he was seized with remorse and returned the thirty pieces of silver to the chief priests and the elders. "I have sinned," he said. "for I have betrayed innocent blood."

"What is that to us?" they replied. "That's your responsibility."

So Judas threw the money into the temple and left. Then he went away and hanged himself.

—Matthew 27:1-5, NIV

Many people talk about Judas betraying Jesus and hanging himself afterward, but not his admission as a sinner. Guilt seized Judas after realizing the condemnation of Jesus, and he returned the money he initially agreed to take. Then, he verbally says that he has sinned.

Jesus chose Judas as he did the other eleven. Judas walked with the Lord experiencing Him and had the opportunity to believe in Him but didn't. The regret of his sin overshadowed his hope of forgiveness. Think for a moment who Judas turned to when he admitted his sin. He turned to the world. He went to the same people--who also allowed Satan to use them--to confess his betrayal. And what did the people say to him? *What is that to us? That's your responsibility* (v4).

Satan is the accuser of the brethren. He accuses us day and night before God (Revelation 12:10). Do you believe for an instant that the enemy was going to forgive Judas for sinning against God? Not for a moment. The devil turned the whole incident around on Judas, and in his accusing way, told Judas that it was all his fault. So, hopeless and defeated, Judas took his own life.

Again, Judas didn't seek forgiveness from God; he sought it from the enemy. And Satan will never oppose himself.

So Jesus called them over to him and began to speak to them in parables: "How can Satan drive out Satan? If a kingdom is divided against itself, that kingdom cannot stand. If a house is divided against itself, that house cannot stand. And if Satan opposes himself and is divided, he cannot stand; his end has come."

—Mark 3:23-26, NIV

Satan will always lead us astray if we turn to the world for forgiveness or answers to spiritual questions. He comes to steal from us, destroy us, and kill us (John 10:10). Remember, our enemy isn't wrapped in flesh and blood; our struggle is with Satan (Ephesians 6:12). If the devil opposes himself, then his end will come. He's well aware of this. So, knowing this truth will set us free, and this realization is how I could forgive my earthly father.

My father consented with the enemy, and I was on the receiving end of this decision. But, like Judas, he recognized his sin. Was I to respond like Satan? No. As a Christian, I forgave my father because Christ has forgiven me.

The enemy will never admit any wrongdoing. Instead, he will turn every decision or accusation back on us. He will also do his best to make it look like it was our idea to betray God. But Jesus equips us with a parable about His Word and the seriousness of holding to the truth so we can send the devil packing.

Equipping Ourselves to Move Forward

"A farmer went out to sow his seed. And as he was scattering the seed, some seed fell along the path, and the birds came and ate it up. Some fell on rocky places, where it did not have much soil. It sprang up quickly, because the soil was shallow. But when the sun came up, the plants were scorched, and they withered because they had no root. Other seed fell among thorns, which grew up and choked the plants. Still other seed fell on good soil, where it produced a crop - a hundred, sixty, or thirty times what was sown. Whoever has ears, let them hear."

—Matthew 13:3-9, NIV

Jesus explains this parable.

"Listen then to what the parable of the sower means: When anyone hears the message about the kingdom and does not understand it, the evil one comes and snatches away what was sown in their heart. This is the seed along the path. The seed falling on rocky ground refers to someone who hears the word and at once receives it with joy. But since they have no root, they last only a short time. When trouble or persecution comes because of the word, they quickly fall away. The seed falling among the thorns refers to someone who hears the word, but the worries of this life and the deceitfulness of wealth choke the word, making it unfruitful. But the seed falling on good soil refers to someone who hears the word and understands it. This is the one who produces a crop, yielding a hundred, sixty or thirty times what was sown."

—Matthew 13:18-23, NIV

Out of the four scenarios, only one produces a crop. The seed is the Word of God, and when it falls on good soil, it yields many times more than what was sown. So how can we hear the Word of God and understand it? We must continue in the Word and ask the Holy Spirit to reveal the truth to us. That's the Spirit's job. Jesus explained the work of the Spirit to His followers before He died on the cross:

"But when, he, the Spirit of truth, comes, he will guide you into all the truth. He will not speak on his own; he will speak only what he hears, and he will tell you what is yet to come."

—John 16:13, NIV

The Spirit takes from what is Christ's and makes His truth known to us (John 13:14). This is why we are able to read scriptures and understand them.

What's the danger in not understanding the Word? Satan will snatch what is sown in our hearts! What's the threat in the seed sown on rocky places? When danger comes, we will quickly fall away because we have no root! What's the danger in the seed sown among thorns? The worries of life choke us, making us unfruitful!

Jesus tells us this so that His joy will be in us, and our joy will be complete (Matthew 15:11). In other words, life without understanding His Word is a life without joy and a life that doesn't produce fruit. It's also one that prevents us from forgiving others.

Very plainly, God tells us to seek Him and live (Amos 5:4).

I encourage you to not merely exist but to seek the Lord and really live. Allow His truth to open your eyes so that you can see and to open your ears so that you can hear. Then, turn towards Him, and trust God to set you free. He is the only One who can. And, together, He can take you to the other side of any storm you face.

Take a moment to worship Him and express your love for His saving grace.

A Prayer for Your Journey:

Lord, thank you for your Word that surpasses my understanding. I may not comprehend everything I read in your scriptures, but I pray, Lord, that your Spirit will give me revelation so that I may know you better. Equip me to turn towards you and not the world so that I can be free. In Jesus' name, I pray, Amen.

A Hymn to Ponder:

Amazing Grace[11]

Song By: Rosemary Siemens

Amazing grace
How sweet the sound
That saved a wretch like me
I once was lost
but now am found
Was blind but now I see

'Twas grace that taught my heart to fear
And grace my fears relieved
How precious did that grace appear
The hour I first believed

When we've been there ten thousand years
Bright shining as the sun
We've no less days to sing God's praise
Then when we first begun

Was blind but now I see

[11] "Most Beautiful Amazing Grace You've EVER Heard! (Rosemary Siemens) (Piano, Voice, Violin)." 2018. www.youtube.com. September 4, 2018. https://www.youtube.com/watch?v=rxuSdBDib-s.

Chapter 7

What is it You Want?

When chains fall from our hands and feet, we experience a freedom in Christ we never have before. Approaching Him becomes familiar, and this freedom provides us the assurance that He'll answer our questions.

In 2018 on a Saturday evening in July, I rushed into the living room to share what the Lord was teaching me, and I grew restless when Josh didn't receive my enthusiasm. As I blabbered away, he just sort of stared into space. Eight long years had passed since baseball ended. Nearly three thousand days of me trying to cheer him up, make him laugh, or dare I say, shift his focus. I was exhausted, and even more so, I was heartbroken over his less than thrilled outlook on life. The boy I married was not the man sitting on the couch next to me that evening.

Honestly, I thought enough time had passed for him to heal. I always heard growing up that time heals wounds. Well, Josh's wounds were still fresh, and if I didn't know any better, I would have thought his dream had died only moments ago. Time was not healing him.

By now, I had tried fixing him many different ways. Mainly, I did my best to shower him with compliments since he'd taken the love language test, and we figured out that words of affirmation are what filled his love tank.[12] I told him over and over that I loved him and that he was a good

---

[12] Chapman, Gary D, and Jocelyn Green. 2017. *The 5 Love Languages: The Secret to Love That Lasts.* Chicago: Northfield Publishing.

father. Our daughter even bought him a key chain that said #1 Dad, but none of us ever saw it hanging from a set of keys.

While sitting in the living room, tears began swelling up in my eyes. I wanted Josh to get excited about the Lord and talking about the Lord. But he wasn't. I was sad, mad, and frustrated all at the same time when out of nowhere I asked him something I never had before. I asked Josh why he never talked to God about what he lost. Why hadn't he asked God why his dream ended? If God's plan included the removal of baseball, then He must have had real reasons for doing so. I know I didn't originally approach Josh to talk about baseball, but in that moment that's what burst out of my mouth.

Why had it taken me so long to pinpoint his hurt? Going back to the time thing, I foolishly believed that Josh would be okay after a few years passed. I also thought that if he had played baseball longer, then he wouldn't have grieved when his career ended. I know now that mindset isn't true. Time does not heal wounds, and more time with your dream doesn't make losing it any easier.

At least my question got his attention. Turning towards me, Josh said he had never questioned God and he didn't know why.

But I did know. It was like someone lifted a veil from my face so I could see more clearly. Josh always accepted whatever came his way. When MLB managers told him he was released, do you know what he said to them time and time again? Thank you. He thanked every manager for giving him a chance when they were the very ones sending him out the door. I mean, could he not have asked a few questions before walking out? No. He never did. That's exactly what he was doing with God. He thanked God for giving him a chance while the weight of his unspoken words crushed his heart. Josh accepted his lot in life without asking God for clarity, and I realized that not knowing why he lost his dream was crippling his life.

Wanting clarity from God is not the same as asking Him for it.

Like Josh, you may have been raised not to question God. As Christians, we believe that God has everything under control, and everything happens for a reason. If we're not careful, these beliefs can prevent us from asking Him about the very thing that hurts us.

Just as time doesn't heal our wounds, neither does avoidance.

Josh talked to God but not about his pain. All along, God knew the hurt inside him and could have brought relief if only Josh had asked. Jesus teaches us the importance of doing just this.

And as they went out of Jericho, a great crowd followed him. And behold, there were two blind men sitting by the roadside, and when they heard that Jesus was passing by, they cried out, "Lord, have mercy on us, Son of David!" The crowd rebuked them, telling them to be silent, but they cried out all the more, "Lord, have mercy on us, Son of David!"
—Matthew 20:29-31, ESV

Imagine needing healing and seeing in the flesh the very one who could heal you. Who of us wouldn't cry out in desperation? Yet, though we acknowledge this truth, we often do not seek the Lord for healing because of the pressure to remain silent. Thankfully, the men in the story ignored such constraints.

First, the men asked Jesus to have mercy on them. That means they wanted forgiveness. Then after the crowd tried to quiet them, the men cried out even louder, begging for forgiveness. Jesus didn't ignore them.

And stopping, Jesus called them and said, "What do you want me to do for you?"
—Matthew 20:32, ESV

Why on Earth would Jesus ask the men what they needed? Didn't He already know? Yes, He did. But Jesus gave them space to ask so they could exercise their faith.

"Lord," they answered, "we want our sight." Jesus had compassion on them and touched their eyes. Immediately they received their sight and followed him.
—Matthew 20:33-34, NIV

The men didn't beat around the bush but asked God for what they needed. In this story, after Jesus heals them, the men immediately follow Him. Begging God for mercy allowed them to confess that only Jesus could save them and asking for healing revealed they believed only Jesus could heal them. Their healing prompted them to follow the Lord.

You may be thinking that you're already following the Lord and asking Him about your loss won't change your commitment to Him. I understand your rationale. If God called you away from your dream, knowing the pain it would bring you, then why should you ask Him about it? But we need to ask God questions we've previously avoided because He wants to heal us. Only God can replace pain with joy that lasts.

After I encouraged Josh to talk to God specifically, I left the room only hoping he would do so. I honestly didn't think he would make such a leap, but amazingly, he did. The following morning, while the kids and I were getting ready for church, Josh went out into the garage and got into our car. He sat in the driver's seat and began conversing with God. Some of his questions are listed below.

Lord, why did baseball end so soon?

Why did you allow me to experience professional baseball if you were going to take it away?

He wanted answers not because they would change his past but because they would change his future. And God answered.

I was unaware that Josh took this step as we headed on to church. The pastor's sermon that morning was about drinking from the living well. As he spoke, God directed Josh to turn to 1 Peter Chapter 5. God didn't verbally tell Josh to open his Bible, but He did put these verses on Josh's heart, which compelled him to turn there. And these are the scriptures he read:

> *To the elders among you, I appeal as a fellow elder and a witness of Christ's sufferings who also will share in the glory to be revealed: Be shepherds of God's flock that is under your care, watching over them—not because you must, but because you are willing, as God wants you to be; not pursuing dishonest gain, but eager to serve; not lording it over those entrusted to you, but being examples to the flock. And when the Chief Shepherd appears, you will receive the crown of glory that will never fade away.*
>
> **—1 Peter 5:1-4, NIV**

First, God told Josh to shepherd the flock under his care by watching over them. Think about that for a moment. Josh is a teacher, he leads the youth at our church, and he voluntarily speaks for FCA. Many aspects of his path involve being an example to young people. Then, God told Josh to be an example, not because he *had* to, but because he was *willing*. God acknowledged the athletic skills He gave Josh, and that baseball didn't end because Josh wasn't physically capable, but He called him away because Josh was willing to go. This calling wasn't for Josh's gain but was meant for him to serve Christ with a further-reaching purpose. And God wanted him to do so with eagerness.

Eagerness involves doing something with enthusiasm and zeal. Goal-setters are typically eager to accomplish tasks for varied reasons, but often it's to attain something. Again, look at what God says in that last scripture. When Jesus appears, those who commit themselves to Him with eagerness to accomplish His work will receive the crown of glory that will never fade. Do you know what the crown of glory is? According to Perry Stone's commentary, the crown of glory is "the type given to the winner of an athletic game. Theologians call this crown the shepherd's crown, awarded at the judgment to faithful pastors, elders, and leaders who loved, taught, and protected the flock in the church."[13]

God told Josh he would receive an athletic crown that would never fade at a time when every other athletic accomplishment in his life *had* faded. Finally, Josh took a drink, and look how the Spirit quenched his thirst!

The intimacy of God's Word still sends chills up my spine. No, God didn't magically erase Josh's memories of baseball to ease his pain. He did something far better. God used His words, to speak directly to one of His children in his time of need. That's why the Bible is called the Living Word. It's alive and active, capable of dividing joints and marrow (Hebrews 4:12). There is no greater medicine on the face of the planet than God's Word. And the Lord is ready to provide the same healing for you.

After Josh read the words of 1 Peter, he reread them several times. Each time he worked to digest the words. And he couldn't wait to share them with me! It was the first time in a long time that I had seen him enthused about anything spiritual. If only he would have asked his question sooner. We have reasons for losing our joy, but we also have a way to regain it.

You haven't done this before. Ask, using my name, and you will receive, and you will have abundant joy.

—John 16:24, NLT

Jesus wants us to ask, in His name, for clarity regarding our pain. No matter the magnitude of our request, Jesus says that we will receive, and our

---

[13] *The Perry Stone Hebraic Prophetic Study Bible, King James Version*. 2016. Fedd Books.

joy will be restored. That's a promise! Galatians 5:22 tells us that joy is a fruit of the Spirit. Christians are capable of producing fruit, but we won't outside God's Word. The more time we spend away from the Lord, the more likely we believe Satan's lies. The enemy will steal whatever he can from us, including our joy.

Do not grieve, for the joy of the Lord is your strength.
—Nehemiah 8:10, NIV

Having joy strengthens us, which means that not having it makes us weak. In this condition, we become more susceptible to the enemy's attacks. But, in Christ, we grow strong and capable of having unexplainable joy amid sorrow. We can delight in the Lord despite our circumstances.

Little by little, I saw Josh's joy begin to surface. He knew he alone couldn't change his situation but allowing God's truth to transcend his understanding brought abiding peace. When we have the peace of God within us, our lack of understanding ceases to torment us because we realize that it's okay not to have all the answers. When God spoke to Josh, He didn't give him a play-by-play of his entire life, but He did provide enough light for Josh to step forward. One step was enough for him to get moving.

Focusing on what could have been, had we not lost our dream, steals our ability to live in the present. Sadly, this focus may last for years, preventing us from ever praising God for what He has made possible.

In an earlier chapter, we discussed the sufferings of Job and the fact that he lost everything when Satan afflicted him. Job initially had a lot to say to God about his situation. Some of his dialogue questioned God's actions but notice how it didn't pinpoint Job's actual pain:

"Why then did you bring me out of the womb? I wish I had died before any eye saw me. Are not my few days almost over? Turn away from me so I can have a moment's joy."
—Job 10:18, 20, NIV

Losing everything caused Job to wish he had never experienced anything. Sound familiar? I've rewritten Job's questions and accompanying thoughts in my own words.

1. Why was I born? (v18)
2. I wish I would have died in the womb. (v18)

3. When is God going to let me die? (v20)
4. God, get away from me so I can have joy. (v20)

Have you ever asked any of these questions or had any of these thoughts? Sometimes our pain can overwhelm us to the point of accusing God rather than seeking His healing. When we think or say these things, we're in danger of unwisely characterizing who God is. So below is what we're actually implying.

1. God made a mistake in creating me. (v18)
2. God doesn't have a real purpose for me. (v18)
3. God should end my life as soon as possible. (v20)
4. God should leave me so I can be happy. (v20)

Of course, we know that the above statements are false. God cannot make mistakes because He is perfect (Matthew 5:48), and He has a purpose for every single one of His creations (Jeremiah 29:11). In addition, we know that apart from the Lord, we cannot have joy because we just previously learned that joy comes from Him (Psalm 16:11).

Beyond questioning our purpose, we may wish we never had a dream or wish we never encountered it. Maybe if we had pursued something else, we would have avoided pain altogether. Not likely. Do you know what this outlook does? It discredits the author of life's ability to give dreams, open doors, and do the impossible. For God has done the impossible in the lives of all His children. Every second of our lives has a purpose.

Later in the book of Job, after he suffers for a time and shares his thoughts, God has much to say to him about his perception:

> *Then the Lord spoke to Job out of the storm. He said: "Who is this that obscures my plans with words without knowledge? Brace yourself like a man; I will question you, and you shall answer me. Where were you when I laid the earth's foundations? Tell me, if you understand. Who marked off its dimensions? Surely you know! Who stretched a measuring line across it? On what were its footings set, or who laid its cornerstone--while the morning stars sang together and all the angels shouted for joy? Surely you know, for you were already born! You have lived so many years!"*
>
> **—Job 38:1-7, 21, NIV**

When I first read these verses, my mouth hung open. Not because I disagreed with the text but because the words put me in my place. Have you ever heard the expression, "You can dish it, but you can't take it?" Well, God's Word can be hard to take, but I like it when He jolts us out of a personal fog.

When we focus on ourselves and all the disappointments we've experienced, we leave little space to stand in reverent awe of God's majesty. God spoke to Job very plainly about his thoughts. Where was Job when God laid the foundations of the Earth? Better yet, where were we? Who marked off the Earth's dimensions or stretched out a measuring line across it? I think we both know the answer. It certainly wasn't us.

Simply put, God grabbed hold of Job and shook him with His words. Can any of us explain God's actions or why He makes the decisions He does? No. We didn't exist when the stars sang and the angels shouted for joy. But notice for a minute in what chapter God says these things. He waited until Chapter 38. That means He allowed Job to get everything off his chest before responding. God would rather us talk to Him than avoid Him because avoidance creates separation. Job suffered, which made him wish he had never been born but thank the Lord he was, or we wouldn't have his story. We wouldn't know the possibility of restored joy after despair.

I encourage you to continue reading Job Chapters 38 through 42. Listen to God's words as He displays His power. We have no idea why God allows certain things to happen, but we also have no idea the impact of our commitment through such storms. There will be people in heaven who came to know Christ because of your commitment to Him when all hope seemed lost. Suffering isn't a destroyer; it tests, refines, and prepares you for God's work.

When Josh lost his dream, he wasn't the only one tested. I, too, was challenged. A couple of years after coming home, it was evident that we would perpetually struggle financially unless we returned to college and finished our degrees. So, Josh returned first to finish his bachelor's degree at EKU, then I did. It wasn't easy. I had no idea what to do with my life outside of being a mom. I felt strange for not having a dream to pursue. Honestly, I envied those who had a plan and were on a mission to complete it.

During this time, Josh considered coaching the baseball team at our alma mater high school. He turned down the offer several times. But even with its challenges, I knew that Josh would be a great coach. I also thought it might be good for him to be around the game and teach young players skills he had learned. Finally, he agreed, and the coaching position led him into teaching. It also led me to the same profession. I never dreamed of becoming a teacher, but I was unaware that God had given me the ability to do so. When the Lord brought us home, the change wasn't only for Josh, it was also for me. I have a purpose to fulfill. And presently, so do you.

God's plans aren't meant to solely benefit us. They are to impact those around us. The Lord created us for a specific time and place. He says so in His Word:

> *From one man he made all the nations, that they should inhabit the whole earth; and he marked out their appointed times in history and the boundaries of their lands. God did this so that they would seek him and perhaps reach out for him and find him, though he is not far from any one of us. For in him we live and move and have our being. As some of your own poets have said, "We are his offspring."*
>
> **—Acts 17:26-28, NIV**

God created us for a specific time and for a particular purpose. He did this so that we would seek Him and reach out to Him. He has given us every opportunity to do so. God also placed us in the communities in which we live to impact His kingdom. People in our paths need to hear our testimonies, see our commitment, and experience our faith. But how many of us are dishonoring our stories? We're trying to forget we ever lived our dream, or we are refusing to use our experiences as platforms. Let's not miss our opportunities to be used by the Lord because others are counting on us.

Your past wasn't an accident, and your present isn't a mistake. To grasp this truth, we must take the first step and ask God about the very thing that's preventing our healing. Let's take this step now.

What is it you want?

Today's Date: ______________________

Say: Lord, I come to you with the pain I have carried for too long. It's crippling my ability to have a life in the present. In Jesus' name, I humbly ask: Why does your will require the loss of my dream?

Now, visualize in your mind what you are specifically asking about.

What you walked away from has impacted your present circumstances and plans. And at this point, you've even made space in your life to accept that God hasn't returned to you what you lost. So, now the question is, why was your life interrupted when you walked with the Lord? He could have prevented it, but He didn't. Knowing this, now the time has come to be still and wait for His Word to transcend your understanding.

He who forms the mountains, who creates the wind, and who reveals his thoughts to mankind, he who turns dawn to darkness, and treads on the high heights of the earth – the Lord God Almighty is his name.

—Amos 4:13, NIV

Allow the Lord to reveal His thoughts to you. As you wait, it's good to remember something else monumental that God didn't prevent. A plan He set in motion before time existed. And nothing or no one stopped it.

Do you remember when God was speaking to Job, and He asked, "*On what were its footings set, or who laid its cornerstone--while the morning stars sang together and all the angels shouted for joy?*" (Job 38:6-7, NIV). Why would stars sing or angels shout for joy because a cornerstone was laid? Because Jesus *is* the cornerstone. He is the foundation upon which our faith stands, and He died on the cross for you and me to inherit eternal life. His purpose included coming to Earth to testify to this truth (John 18:37).

We have reasons for being here on Earth as well. In order to carry out those reasons, it's vital that we receive healing from the Lord.

Growing in our faith is why we must go to the Father and ask Him to fill the void in our lives that we've lived with but not dealt with. It's time to address the pain that has worn us down. Then, we must listen to His voice and believe what He tells us. He is our friend and waits for us to carry everything to Him in prayer.

Record God's Answer Here:

When God answers your prayer and gives you clarity regarding your situation, I want you to return to this page and write down His words below. You may receive your answer soon or it may take some time, but regardless of the wait, writing down what the Lord tells you will provide you clarity for years to come.

Date: ____________________________

____

____

____

____

____

____

____

____

____

A Prayer for Your Journey:

Lord, thank you for listening to my prayers. I know that you hear me, and I ask you to forgive me for not always being transparent. I believe that you will answer my request in time. May you open my ears and ready my heart to receive your response. I love you. In Jesus' name, I pray, Amen.

A Hymn to Ponder:

What a Friend We Have in Jesus[14]

Written By: Joseph Scriven
Song By: Alan Jackson

What a friend we have in Jesus,
All our sins and griefs to bear!
What a privilege to carry
Everything to God in prayer!

What a peace we often forfeit,
O what needless pain we bear,
All because we do not carry
Everything to God in prayer.

Have we trials and temptations?
Is there trouble anywhere?
We should never be discouraged,
Take it to the Lord in prayer.

Can we find a friend so faithful
Who will all our sorrows share?
Jesus knows our every weakness,
Take it to the Lord in prayer.

---

14 "Alan Jackson - What a Friend We Have in Jesus (Live)." 2017. www.youtube.com. August 25, 2017. https://www.youtube.com/watch?v=znWu2HCJ92c.

Chapter 8

As a Deer Pants for Water

When Josh's baseball career ended, memories of what used to be stared at me daily in our home. Of course, most people do not have a rack of baseball bats hanging in their houses, and if they did, the memorabilia probably wouldn't emanate grief. But for me, there was a period where each time I looked at Josh's jerseys, baseball bats, gloves, or pictures, I got sad. I immediately thought of the hurtful times in Josh's career rather than the good. More than anything, I wished Josh's career had gone the way he wanted so his thirst for the game wasn't in vain.

You may have struggled with something like this. Have you ever looked at something in your house and got sad? Or angry or bitter? Sometimes our minds focus on what is negative rather than positive. Yet, we must work to do the opposite, and we can't do it alone (John 15:5). God instructs us to always think about what is good in life.

Finally, brothers and sisters, whatever is true, whatever is noble, whatever is right, whatever is pure, whatever is lovely, whatever is admirable – if anything is excellent or praiseworthy – think about such things.
—Philippians 4:8, NIV

The Lord desires us to think about what is true, noble, right, pure, lovely, and admirable because all these things come from Him. I believe that God deliberately tells us to think about praiseworthy things because He knows how much our minds wander. We have no reason to allow the hurt in our lives to overshadow the good. Thankfully, God equips all believers with the Spirit to see good in everything--no matter how devastating.

For example, the Lord is using me to write the words you are reading during a most difficult trial. Receiving chemotherapy treatment for breast cancer is both physically and emotionally draining. My immunity is low, and if I'm not careful, my sentiment will be as well. But rather than focus on the negative, I pray for good days because of the intimate time I get to spend with my Savior. I look forward to my time with Him because He fills me with wisdom and words to share with you.

Hearing from the Lord requires us to spend more time pursuing Him than we do dwelling on our unfavorable situations. Therefore, after asking God about our pain, our next step is to seek Him and truly live (Amos 5:4). In the book of Psalm, we have an image of what it means to thirst for the Lord:

As the deer pants for streams of water, so my soul pants for you, my God. My soul thirsts for God, for the living God. When can I go and meet with God?

—Psalm 42:1-2, NIV

Have you ever asked when you can meet with God? Or has your soul ever panted for Him? Panting for something means gasping for it or being breathless without it. I can't say I have ever seen a deer pant for water, but I certainly have seen dogs do this. After running around a yard or field, dogs pant for water and are desperate for it. Water quenches their thirst and allows their bodies to cool down. And then, most often, they can be still and relaxed.

The same is true of us. God is our living water, and we need Him every day to quench our spiritual thirst. To better understand what it means to *seek* the Lord, I've turned the word into an acronym to help guide us.

S - Start with the Spirit

God promises us that when we seek Him with all our hearts, we find Him (Jeremiah 29:13). Going after Him, then, means we acknowledge where He lives. As Christians, His Spirit lives within us, so our search for God begins inwardly as we communicate with Him. We do this by talking to the Lord or praying. Even when we don't know how to put our prayer into words, the Spirit intercedes for us (Romans 8:26). He takes what we can't express and aligns our thoughts with the will of God. As we spend time with the Lord, we can start to follow His leading if we're intentional. His footprints are all around us, but if we're distracted, we'll miss them. When Christ called His first disciples to follow Him, they walked away from something. So it is with us. He also requires that we leave behind things that hinder us from moving forward.

> *Therefore, since we are surrounded by such a huge crowd of witnesses to the life of faith, let us strip off every weight that slows us down, especially the sin that so easily trips us up. And let us run with endurance the race God has set before us.*
>
> **—Hebrews 12:1, NLT**

The question is, what's hindering us? God says it is a sin to know what you ought to do and then not do it (James 4:17). In the life of a believer, this means knowing we should follow Christ and then choosing not to--is sin. If we're not careful, inward emotions can cause us to sin, preventing us from doing the very thing that allows us to live. And that is seeking Christ.

For a time in my Christian walk, misperceptions hindered my faith. I honestly believed that my commitment to the Lord meant that "everything would work out." Adding to these words, what I'm more suggesting is that everything would work out for me. Or everything would work out for my husband. When his baseball career began to unravel, I was desperate for Christ, even to the point of panicking in prayer for Him to restore Josh's career. That type of desperation is not what it means to thirst for God. I was thirsting for the good of myself. But I believed that's what I was supposed to do. I was supposed to pray really hard, and then wait for God to fix everything. Unfortunately, that's a partial truth.

The Lord does instruct us to pray about everything, but our moments of panic during prayer will not get us what we want. Panicking for God is not the same thing as panting for Him.

God causes everything to work together for the good of those who love the Lord and are called according to His purpose. Romans 8:28 is quoted to encourage people, but the second part of the verse is often neglected. More plainly, the stroke of God's hand doesn't wipe away every trial, but He does bring good even from bad situations. And this good is for those who love Him. Loving Him means we throw off what hinders us and obey His principles. That's when we begin to thirst for Him rather than ourselves.

As a deer pants for water, thirsting for the Lord is to desire Him above anything else. Above our wants, dreams, hurts, and disappointments. In other words, if all we have is Christ, then He's enough. The more time we spend with Him, the easier it is to recognize His guidance.

"My sheep listen to my voice; I know them, and they follow me."
—John 10:27, NIV

Simply put, it's impossible to follow the Lord without hearing His voice. The Spirit guides believers daily by nudging them to do *this* or warning them not to do *that.* Therefore, we must be sensitive to His instruction to stay on the right path. God doesn't tell us to try any path before us, but rather the opposite.

So be careful to do what the Lord your God has commanded you; do not turn aside to the right or to the left.
—Deuteronomy 5:32, NIV

There is a path that God is leading *you* down. That's the one to follow. But unfortunately, we don't always stick to God's plans when we're weary. In the Old Testament, the Israelites could relate to this. When the Lord initially led the Israelites out of Egypt, notice His rationale for choosing the best route:

When Pharaoh let the people go, God did not lead them on the road through the Philistine country, though that was shorter. For God said, "If they face war, they might change their minds and return to Egypt." So God led the people around by the desert road toward the Red Sea.
—Exodus 13:17-18, NIV

These verses show us that the shortest path is not always best. God did not want the Israelites to be in a situation where they may have changed their minds, so He took them along the desert road toward the Red Sea. That's where He performed a miracle in front of their eyes. Rather than face war, God's people walked across the Red Sea on dry land. Initially leaving Egypt, God knew they weren't ready for war, but later, as their faith increased, they would be. Wouldn't you like to see what the Lord has spared you from? God leads us one place and takes us around another for the sake of His glory and our good.

During the forty years that the Israelites spent in the desert, there were times that they listened to God, and then there were times they did not.

Their impatience often led to calamity. When their leader, Moses, went up to Mount Sinai to meet with the Lord, he was gone for an extended period of time. In this meeting, God gave Moses the Ten Commandments and many other daily living laws. But take notice of the Israelite's actions in Moses' absence:

When the people saw that Moses was so long in coming down from the mountain, they gathered around Aaron and said, "Come, make us gods who will go before us. As for this fellow Moses who brought us up out of Egypt, we don't know what has happened to him."
—Exodus 32:1, NIV

Aaron, Moses' brother, gave in to the people's demands and assisted them in making a golden calf to worship. Because of their impatience, three thousand people later died (Exodus 32:28). What did God have to say about their actions? First, they forgot Him, next, they were impatient, and finally, they didn't believe His words.

But they soon forgot what he had done and did not wait for his plan to unfold. Then they despised the pleasant land; they did not believe his promise.
—Psalm 106:13, 24, NIV

May we never forget what God has done for us during our restlessness or most significant trials. If we take a moment to consider the hand of God in our lives, it doesn't take long for a list of blessings to form. His favor encircles us, and daily His miracles are on display.

E - Every Day Have Conversations

As we begin to seek the Lord and thirst for Him, others will notice. We may even look weird or silly at times in the eyes of those around us. Take heart, because in these moments, we are showing that though we are in the world, we are not of it. Furthermore, we are letting the world know that greater is He that is in us than he that is in the world (1 John 4:4). And talking about the Lord in everyday conversations will not be strange. God tells us to do just that.

Love the Lord your God with all your heart and with all your soul and with all your strength. These commandments that I give you today are to be on your hearts. Impress them on your children. Talk about them when you sit at home and when you walk along the road, when you lie down and when you get up. Tie them as symbols on your hands and bind them on your foreheads.

Write them on the doorframes of your houses and on your gates.
—Deuteronomy 6:5-9, NIV

If I talk about the Lord when I sit, walk, lie down, and get up, when would I not talk about Him? And if I am in constant conversation about the Lord, then my children should hear and be a part of such discussions. This is something Josh and I strive to do in our home. We make a point to teach our children the ways of the Lord because it's our responsibility to train them (Proverbs 22:6). Over time, then, conversing about the Lord becomes the norm rather than the exception.

People will start to see our faith and not our doubts. In the book of Acts, after boldly proclaiming the gospel of Christ, people took notice of Peter and John's faith. In front of the elders, teachers of the law, and the high priest, Peter declared that salvation is found in Christ alone.

When they saw the courage of Peter and John and realized that they were unschooled, ordinary men, they were astonished and they took note that these men had been with Jesus.
—Acts 4:13, NIV

May those around us take note that we have been with Jesus as well! Our education is irrelevant. What matters is our commitment to follow and spend time with our Savior. The more time we spend with the Lord, the more sensitive we'll become to the Spirit's proddings, knowing when to do something and when not to. Don't be surprised when God changes your direction. Even if your circumstance changes, your purpose will not. There are plenty of instances in the Bible where God changed the course of His followers even after directing them to a particular region.

When Jesus was born in Bethlehem, Magi traveled to greet Him from the east. They approached King Herod and asked where the King of the Jews was born. Of course, this disturbed King Herod because he wanted this so-called king dead. But rather than show his wickedness, he told the Magi to find the King of the Jews and to report back His exact location. That way, King Herod could supposedly worship this ruler. After leaving King Herod, the star guided the Magi to where Jesus was born. But the men didn't return home the way they came.

And having been warned in a dream not to go back to Herod, they returned to their country by another route.
—Matthew 2:12, NIV

After the Magi left to return to their country, an angel of the Lord spoke to Joseph, the earthly father of Jesus, in a dream.

"Get up," he said, "take the child and his mother and escape to Egypt. Stay there until I tell you, for Herod is going to search for the child to kill him."
—Matthew 2:13, NIV

If we are not sensitive to God's voice, we will miss important instructions and guidance. In this space, most often, we will endure hardship. What if the Magi had returned to King Herod? What if Joseph and Mary didn't take Jesus to Egypt? Thankfully they obeyed by recognizing God's voice in a dream. Dreams are one way God speaks to His followers. He also speaks His Word to us as we read the Bible, and He uses other believers to deliver His messages. His Word never returns void but always accomplishes the purpose for which it is sent (Isaiah 55:11).

As we grow in our faith, we will learn to recognize God's voice and trust His Words. Then, we will begin to act on what the Lord tells us despite the opinions of others. Have you ever obeyed God and then told someone you made your decision based on what God told you to do? Initially, this may feel strange, but obeying the Lord's calling is the most protective space we can occupy. One person that can attest to this is Noah. He lived on Earth during a time of significant corruption.

So God said to Noah, "I am going to put an end to all people, for the earth is filled with violence because of them. I am surely going to destroy both them and the earth. So make yourself an ark of cypress wood; make rooms in it and coat it with pitch inside and out."
—Genesis 6:13-14, NIV

Notice God said, "make *yourself* an ark." The task in front of Noah, if he followed through, was designed to save his life. And the vessel did. The ark was built on dry land and was 450 feet long, 75 feet wide, and 45 feet high (Genesis 6:15). That's humongous! The only way the ark could lift off the ground was by the floodwaters that God sent. Noah had to believe the floodwaters would come at a time when it had never rained on Earth (Genesis 2:5-6). Can you imagine the backlash Noah received during this period? Especially when the Earth was full of violence and corrupt people. But Noah walked with God, and he believed His words.

Noah did everything just as God commanded him.
—Genesis 6:22, NIV

Noah trusted God's voice, and he obeyed the Lord regardless of the insults hurled at him. And what was the consequence of his obedience? He and his family, along with many animals, were saved.

Sometimes faith will make us look foolish until it starts to rain.

In my walk with the Lord, there have certainly been times when Josh and I felt a little crazy for taking specific actions. A primary example is when we came home from baseball because the Lord told us to. Baseball was all Josh had ever known, and to many people, he looked silly for not trying to play longer. Another instance is when the Lord called me to write the very words you're reading. I had never written anything notable and didn't understand why God wanted me to write a book. Plenty of people have given me blank stares for even mentioning such a calling over the years. But all the doubts faded when I began to feel drops of water falling on my skin. God is faithful, and no matter how many promises He's made, they are Yes in Christ (2 Corinthians 1:20). We only need to be obedient to what He's called us to do. And talking to Him daily keeps us yearning for the rain.

E - Eagerly Hope in God's Word

I've often heard that people should "step out and find out" if they're confused about which way to turn. Don't get me wrong, life requires us to be risk-takers at times, but we can avoid heaps of turmoil if we learn to listen to God's voice and wait for His guidance. A couple of years after Josh's baseball career ended, he experienced a period of "stepping out and finding out" to see if he could use his gifts in other areas. Within a short period of time, Josh opened a baseball hitting facility and ran for public office. Both decisions required significant time and financial commitments. Yet, in and of themselves, these decisions appeared harmless. But God didn't tell us to make either of these decisions. They were good ideas, but not God's ideas. So, neither one of them worked out as we'd hoped. And what choice were we left with? We were either going to believe God's promises for our lives or not believe them. This required us to hate every wrong path.

I gain understanding from your precepts; therefore I hate every wrong path.
You are my refuge and my shield; I have put my hope in your word.
—Psalm 119: 104, 114, NIV

Eagerly putting our hope in God's Word is perhaps the most important step in seeking the Lord. We know that hope rooted in the Lord does not disappoint us. God's Word is flawless without any errors, so putting our hope there is the safest place (Psalm 18:30). And as we trust what He says, we'll begin to follow His ways over our own. Even when His methods seem to move at a snail's pace, we need to remember God is not slow in keeping His promises.

The Lord is not slow in keeping his promise, as some understand slowness. Instead he is patient with you, not wanting anyone to perish, but everyone to come to repentance.

—2 Peter 3:9, NIV

When we think we are the ones being patient with God, He is actually the one being patient with us. Why? Because He knows what we're ready for and what we're not prepared for. Scripture says that God waited on Noah to finish the ark (1 Peter 3:20). Not the other way around. His patience meant Noah's salvation. He knows what is truly best for us at each stage of our lives. Good ideas are all around us, and the world portrays a very selfish path along the route to what it perceives as success. Where the world tells us to make ourselves happy, the Lord instructs us to seek Him, and He will give us everything we need (Matthew 6:33).

The Lord directs the steps of the godly. He delights in every detail of their lives. Though they stumble, they will never fall, for the Lord holds them by the hand.

—Psalm 37:23-24, NLT

It is comforting to know that God takes pleasure in every aspect of our lives. There is nothing in our lives too small or insignificant for Him to ignore. Even though we stumble at times, we will never completely fall when we follow the Lord because He is directing our steps. And He isn't the only one who adores such communion.

Direct me in the path of your commands, for there I find delight.

—Psalm 119:35, NIV

When we seek the Lord, we too have delight. In other words, we obtain joy, happiness, and excitement by following Him. But the conditions of our hearts must be open to what God has for us in order for us to acquire such delight. If we're not careful, years of pain can cause our hearts to grow hard or calloused.

K - Know Your Heart's Condition

See to it, brothers and sisters, that none of you has a sinful, unbelieving heart that turns away from the living God. But encourage one another daily, as long as it is called "Today," so that none of you may be hardened by sin's deceitfulness.

—Hebrews 3:12-13, NIV

Sin is misleading and hides the truth. When sin's deceitfulness hardens our hearts, we are in danger of turning away from the Lord rather than following Him. Calloused hearts form over time as layers of hurt build up within us.

While playing professional baseball, Josh kept callouses on his hands. They wouldn't go away because he never stopped training. He repeated the same motion of swinging a bat over and over. I remember touching the rough areas and feeling how hard they were. He even told me that if he poked the callouses with a knife, he wouldn't feel any pain. Likewise, if our hearts get to this point--numb from the pain we've experienced--we're in danger of lacking feeling. And when we stop feeling, we stop caring. At this point, delighting in the Lord becomes a far and distant concept.

Having a hard heart means we lack understanding.

One such story clearly defines this truth. In Mark's account, Jesus performed a miracle by feeding five thousand people with only five loaves of bread and two fish. He had compassion on the great crowd of people in front of Him because they were like sheep without a shepherd. Initially, Jesus' disciples told Him to send the people away into the nearby villages to get food, but the Lord responded with an astonishing statement:

But he answered, "You give them something to eat."

—Mark 6:37, NIV

The disciples refuted such a statement. They explained that feeding that many people would take eight months of a man's wages. Did Jesus really want them to spend that much money? No. Instead, Christ called them to action:

"How many loaves do you have?" he asked. "Go and see."
—Mark 6:38, NIV

After figuring out how much bread and fish they had, the disciples reported to Jesus the numbers: five loaves and two fish. Jesus then took the food and held it up towards heaven, giving thanks and breaking the loaves. Every single person in attendance ate, and there were even twelve basketfuls of broken pieces of food leftover. The Lord performed a miracle in front of His followers by using what *they* had. He isn't asking us for anything more than what we have either. Jesus only wants our believing hearts.

Directly after this event, Jesus had His disciples get into a boat and travel on to another area while He dismissed the crowd. From the shore of the water, He saw His disciples straining at the oars because the wind was against them. So, He went out to them, walking on the water. When His disciples saw Him, they cried out in terror, thinking Jesus was a ghost.

Immediately he spoke to them and said, "Take courage! It is I. Don't be afraid." Then he climbed into the boat with them, and the wind died down. They were completely amazed, for they had not understood about the loaves; their hearts were hardened.
—Mark 6:50-52, NIV

This time Jesus spoke first to His followers instead of the wind. He told them to take courage and not be afraid while He was standing on the water. The wind was blowing against the boat when Jesus spoke the words. It wasn't until after the Lord climbed in that the wind died down. So why were the disciples amazed? Their hearts were hardened, and they lacked understanding. When they saw Jesus walking on water, they still hadn't understood the previous lesson about the loaves. And the lesson is this: God uses a believing heart offered to Him in faith. Such fertile ground produces a crop many times more than what was sown (Matthew 13:8).

If we're not careful, our calloused hearts can cause us to miss what God has in store for us. We may forget His miracles, wisdom, revelation, and insight. Sometimes, like the disciples, we're even shocked if something good happens to us, as if we don't recognize the author of such comfort. Instead, we might attribute such occurrences as luck, dismissing altogether that God delights in every single detail of our lives. And He desires that we delight in Him as well. We are His sheep, and He is our shepherd, directing each of our steps.

The good news is that we don't have to keep a calloused heart. When we commit to seeking the Lord with all our being, He gives us a new heart.

I will give you a new heart and put a new spirit in you; I will remove from you your heart of stone and give you a heart of flesh.
—Ezekiel 36:26, NIV

It's not God's will that any should perish, and that includes His children who grow calloused from a hard heart. We are never too far from God to obtain restoration. All we must do is ask the Lord to renew a loyal heart within us (Psalm 51:10).

So let us run our race with endurance, thirsting for God as a deer pants for water. He will never let the righteous fall (Psalm 55:22).

A Prayer for Your Journey:

Lord, I desire you more than the world. I've learned that obeying your commands is where I find delight. Help me run the race you planned for me before the foundations of the world were laid. Though trials have tossed me about, I come to you just as I am. In Jesus' name, I pray, Amen.

A Hymn to Ponder:

Just As I Am[15]

Song by: Jason Crabb

I've been trying to figure out
what it means to be human
flesh and bone
The Spirit and the soul

If I can not earn Your love
By trying to measure up
Why do I think I'd lose it in the lows?

Somehow You see through my heart
And You welcome me with open arms

Just as I am
In the good and the bad
You still understand
And You never stop loving me
Just as I am
With the heart of the Father
And grace like no other
You never stopped loving me
Just as I am

You've been patient with my wandering
Always knowing what I need
With a gentle hand
You show me where to go

No there hasn't been a moment
You were calling out to me
I heard Your voice and now

---

[15] "Jason Crabb - Just as I Am (Official Lyric Video)." 2021. www.youtube.com. February 10, 2021. https://www.youtube.com/watch?v=xdstMOPLnbY.

I'm coming home

Just as I am
In the good and the bad
You still understand
That You never stop loving me
Just as I am
With the heart of the Father
And grace like no other
Oh You never stopped loving me
Just as I am

I just want to say
Thank you, thank you
Thank you for loving me

I just want to say
Thank you, thank you
Thank you for loving me

I just want to say
Thank you, thank you
Thank you for loving me

I just want to say
Thank you, thank you
Thank you for loving me

Just as I am
In the good and the bad
You still understand
Oh You never stop loving me
Just as I am
With the heart of the Father
And grace like no other
You never stopped loving me
Just as I am
Just as I am

Chapter 9

A Seat at His Table

Knowing that God delights in every single detail of our lives (Psalm 37:23) means that He's concerned with how we use our time. When my chemotherapy treatments began, I decided to take off work to get the rest I needed and better manage the side effects. I initially thought going to work was doable, as some cancer patients do continue their regular routines, but I realized that I couldn't keep the pace I had before. When I explained this decision to my principal at the elementary school where I work, she immediately jumped into action and created a meal train for the staff to help provide meals for my family.

Due to my principal's actions, someone knocks on my door with food nearly every day. It's hard to explain what this means to me or the feeling I get when I see one of my coworkers pull into the driveway. Each of them is intentional to drive out into the country where I live and bring nourishment to my family. They don't have to come, but they choose to. They knock on my door even when it's inconvenient for them.

And as I journey down the path God has placed before me, I now better understand His words when He says to the faithful that He shows Himself faithful (2 Samuel 22:26). In one of my most significant hours of need, the Lord is providing in a critical way. He is using the community around me to bring my family comfort. This unforeseen act of compassion reminds me daily that God will never forget His children, no matter the situation they're in.

Can a mother forget the baby at her breast and have no compassion on the child she has born? Though she may forget, I will not forget you! See, I have engraved you on the palms of my hands; your walls are ever before me.

—Isaiah 49:15-16, NIV

Most assuredly, the Lord used the analogy of a mom with her baby because of their shared intimacy. After nourishing a child for months within her womb, the day finally comes when the child is born, and the mom sets eyes on the new life for the first time. Then she holds her baby's skin against her own. Within this scene, it's difficult for any of us to imagine that same mom forgetting her child. Honestly, it seems impossible. But God tells us that even if that does happen, He will never forget us. We need to mark this truth down: we are unforgettable to our Creator!

God's love for us extends beyond our imaginations. This certainty is why we seek Him, because the world will never love us as He does. I wish to have reminded myself of this fact for all the years I spent frustrated about my husband's baseball career. Should I have expected the world to love and appreciate Josh's talent as God did? Why did I sink such confidence in a game if it's possible for a mom to forget the baby at her breast? Unless you and I are of the world, the world will never love us. But that's ok. We belong to Christ, and He has already overcome the world (John 16:33).

Seeking worldly love, then, is a dead-end path. The journey may appear enticing, but the result is always disappointing.

By contrast, our commitment to the Lord allows Him to broaden the path beneath us so that our ankles do not turn (2 Samuel 22:37). Therefore, we need not fear what will become of our devotion to Him or what we'll encounter along the way. Instead, seeking God is exactly what we are supposed to do because, again, those who hope in Him will never be disappointed (Isaiah 49:23).

Keep on asking, and you will receive what you ask for. Keep on seeking, and you will find. Keep on knocking, and the door will be opened to you. For everyone who asks, receives. Everyone who seeks, finds. And to everyone who knocks, the door will be opened."

—Matthew 7:7-8, NLT

At this point in our journey, we have asked God about our pain, and the importance of seeking Him is more apparent because we've learned that we will find Him when we seek Him with all our hearts (Jeremiah 29:13).

Now, the next step is for us to knock on His door. And each of these steps is continuous because the Lord tells us to keep on doing them. We need Him every second of our lives, so there will never be a time that we quit asking, seeking, or knocking. But what does it mean to *knock*?

Picture a special friend pulling into your driveway and walking up to your front door. This friend has journeyed to see your face and spend time with you. Upon arrival, your friend sees where you live, broadening his perspective of you so that he can understand you better. As he knocks on your door, you open it to find your friend has something to share with you. And together, you fellowship with one another. Maintaining a friendship shows dedication but knocking on your friend's door reveals a desire to share in their life.

Many years ago, my husband and I traveled to Memphis, Tennessee, to see my childhood friend. Her son was diagnosed with leukemia, and the only thing I could think to do was get in my car and go and see her. Walking through the St. Joseph Children's Hospital changed my life as I passed by many children sick with cancer. When we arrived at my friend's door, I threw my arms around her. Did her face light up because I could change her son's diagnosis? No. She was comforted by a friend who traveled to see her. And I wanted to be there if only for a moment, to share in what she and her family were experiencing.

Fast forward ten years, and that same friend was knocking on my door. She and her family traveled to see me when she heard the news of my breast cancer diagnosis. She threw her arms around me and spent time sharing my experience. No, she couldn't physically change my situation, but she and her husband could undoubtedly be there for Josh and me, praying for God's healing touch.

Knocking on His Door

When we knock on the Lord's door, we acknowledge that we've received His Words and are ready to partake in them. We agree with Him regarding where He has us and desire to sit at His table. And like a good friend, when we knock, His door always opens. He wants us to dine with Him because the meal He's prepared is for us. Christ is among us as one who serves, and we stand by Him as witnesses of His sacrifice for us. So, as we partake, He breaks the bread and gives thanks. Then He tells us that the bread is His body given to us. Likewise, He takes the cup and tells us that it represents the promise of His blood poured out for us (Luke 22:19-20).

Christ didn't only give up His body for us--He poured Himself out. That means He withheld nothing from us. We can relax then and dine at His table because we can trust Him. Unless we knock, we cannot share in His sufferings so that we may share in His glory.

And as we dine with the Lord, may we become still and know that He is God (Psalm 46:10). We will never fully embrace Him unless we become still. Calming ourselves in time spent with Him is needed for our anxieties to vanish and for an unwavering faith to usher in. Roots begin to grow and anchor our souls to have a firm place to stand during our darkest hours. What is the result of our being still and knowing God is who He says He is?

Stand firm, and you will win life.
—Luke 21:19, NIV

That life is a promise for when we die, but it's also a promise for the present. Life is not worth living unless we have purpose and contentment. Both come from spending time with the Lord and allowing Him to fill us with good things. And in His presence is when we start believing in His goodness despite what we experienced along the path to Him. Earlier when I described my decision to take off work while undergoing chemotherapy, I did so with the intentions of getting physical rest. During this time my body wasn't the only thing that was still – my mind was as well. What I thought was time off to heal, God revealed that it was time for me to get still. And in His presence came the words you are now reading.

How kind the Lord is! How good he is! So merciful, this God of ours! The Lord protects those of childlike faith; I was facing death, and he saved me. Let my soul be at rest again, for the Lord has been good to me.
—Psalm 116:5-7, NLT

Resting in the Lord occurs when we truly believe that He has been good to us.

Physical rest is soothing but spiritual rest is freeing. When our souls can rest from the worries and anxieties of this life, we can be at ease knowing God is who He says He is. Nothing can separate us from the love of God that is in Christ Jesus (Romans 8:39). The moments we share with

Him, reclining at His table, cannot be taken from us. And as we share in the meal that He has prepared for us, let's take in the fullness of Him. We are not there to sample the fruits of His vine; we are there to experience each course.

To encounter such freedom, we must once again consider the condition of our hearts. Enjoying the Lord's meal means we must be thankful for what He's prepared for us, even if we don't like some of the food. We've all been there before, sitting at a dinner table eager to eat, when suddenly we see a side dish we don't care for. And rather than be impolite, we cleverly bypass the dish without mentioning our distaste. Not so with the Lord. Each course of His meal is for us, and to better know Him is to share in each one. We cannot avoid parts of the meal we do not like because we choose to ignore what the Lord has for us.

Disregarding parts of God's meal paints a one-sided picture of Him. This view leads to questions such as, how could a good God allow this or that to happen? Have you ever asked that question or heard someone else ask it? Trials that we experience evoke emotions that may lead us to such inquiries. Most often, when we place blame on the Lord, we haven't taken in the fullness of Him. We may taste His love but bypass His justice. Or we may indulge in His mercy without considering our sin's accountability.

The Lord has already shown us what is good. So, what does He require of us? We are to be fair and show compassion while walking humbly with Him (Micah 6:8).

Recently, I woke up to a white blanket of snow covering the ground and trees. The sight outside my bedroom window was beautiful. I couldn't see a blade of grass in the yard, and for a moment, I stared at the stunning landscape. However, when my daughter woke up, she was less than enthused. Yes, she was excited about the snow, but not about staying home. She complained and complained about not getting to go to her friend's house. At one point, she got so upset that she yelled across the house, "I don't know why God made it snow anyway. I thought He was a nice man!" Of course, I can laugh at her comment because it's a very childish one. She was upset because she couldn't enjoy the snow with her friend. We say silly things when we are young, but we gain maturity and awareness of our words as we grow older.

It's the same in our daily walk with Christ. When we knock on His door to fellowship with Him, it's time for us to get off spiritual milk and move on to solid food.

Anyone who lives on milk, being still an infant, is not acquainted with the teaching about righteousness. But solid food is for the mature, who by constant use have trained themselves to distinguish good from evil.
—Hebrews 5:13-14, NIV

If solid food is for the mature, then that is what I want. I do not desire to suck on a bottle of spiritual milk when there is a plate of food within my grasp. These delicacies are for us who leave the elementary teachings of Christ and move on to maturity. The foundation has been laid. If we keep laying the same foundation over and over again in our Christian walk, then our houses will never be built. When the storms of life come, we'll have nothing to protect us because unwavering faith is what builds strong walls, constructs a sturdy roof, and provides windows and doors. Our houses, or bodies, are designed to eat solid food, holding firmly to the faith we profess because we have a high priest who can sympathize with us in our weaknesses. Christ was tempted in every way yet was without sin (Hebrews 4:14-15).

Since Jesus was tempted in every way, nothing in our spiritual baggage needs dismissing. Therefore, whatever is weighing us down can be freely discussed.

Let us then approach God's throne of grace with confidence, so that we may receive mercy and find grace to help us in our time of need.
—Hebrews 4:16, NIV

While on Earth, Jesus Himself offered up prayers and petitions with cries to the one who could save Him from death (Hebrews 5:7). How much more so should we approach His throne with confidence, knowing that He hears us? The Lord will always help us in our time of need because He understands the necessity. Although Jesus walked the Earth as the Son of God, He learned obedience from what He suffered (Hebrews 5:8). That obedience comes to us in the form of solid food. As we model the same devotion as Christ, we begin to eat the solid food that provides sustaining nourishment to our souls.

Unwavering faith in the Lord also brings enjoyment and fulfillment. We can discover happiness amid sorrow and acquire joy within sadness because having an unshakable faith means we've made our hope sure. Such devotion urges us to keep going regardless of the obstacles standing in our way.

When Josh left the minor leagues to join the Houston Astros, he had a manager who believed in him. That may sound strange because don't all coaches believe in their players? Yes, but this situation was unique. The confidence placed in Josh wasn't a secret held by his manager but rather made known through words and actions. Josh once told me that he would "run through a wall" for a coach who believed in him. In Houston, that's exactly what he did. The Lord created an environment that allowed Josh to have success, and a big part of that circumstance was blessing Josh with a leader who valued his skills. Josh was given playing time as a young rookie and was verbally encouraged to use the abilities that got him to where he was. The result of such actions allowed Josh to rest in his craft. The notion that he could use what he had on the field to help his team created the best month of baseball Josh ever played in the big leagues. His coach believed in him, and the results were lasting.

Believing Into Maturity

Just as Josh believed his manager's words, we must also believe what the Lord tells us as we dine with Him. A message from the Lord will be useless to us unless we combine the words with our faith (Hebrews 4:2). Otherwise, His words are of no value to us. We must pay careful attention to what we have heard so that we do not drift away (Hebrews 2:1).

When we don't believe what God tells us, we stay infants in Christ. As a result, we keep sucking on a bottle when we should be eating solid food. An excellent example of this is in the book of Luke on the day of Christ's resurrection.

On the third day, after Christ's crucifixion, women went to the tomb bringing spices they had prepared. However, when they entered the tomb, they did not find Jesus' body which caused them to wonder what happened. Two angels appeared to them and reminded them of what Christ said as they considered the events.

The Son of Man must be delivered over to the hands of sinners, be crucified, and on the third day be raised again.

—Luke 24:7, NIV

Upon hearing these words, the women then remembered. They went back and told all of what they heard and saw to the eleven disciples. The men did not believe their words because it seemed like foolishness. Peter, however, got up and went to the tomb. He saw the strips of linen lying by themselves and went away wondering what had happened (Luke 24:9-12).

The question is, should any of Christ's followers have wondered what happened to Jesus? No. The Lord told them repeatedly before He died what was going to happen. Truthfully, on the third day after His death, all His disciples should have run to the tomb expecting it to be empty. I realize it's easy for us to make such assumptions on this side of the cross. We have God's Word in front of us to read and meditate on daily. We know the end from the beginning.

But how many of us still wonder about things God has already explained? Just like Cleopas, Jesus must reexplain His words to us to extinguish our doubts.

On the same resurrection day, two men were traveling to Emmaus. As they discussed all that took place in Jerusalem, suddenly, Jesus came up walking alongside them. They didn't recognize His presence among them as Jesus asked them what they were discussing. This question prompted the men to stand still, lowering their faces.

One of them, named Cleopas, asked him, "Are you the only one visiting Jerusalem who does not know the things that have happened there in these days?" "What things?" he asked.

—Luke 24:18-19, NIV

I find it funny that Jesus acted as if He didn't know what happened. But He allowed the men to testify who He was.

"About Jesus of Nazareth," they replied. "He was a prophet, powerful in word and deed before God and all the people. The chief priests and our rulers handed him over to be sentenced to death, and they crucified him; but we had hoped that he was the one who was going to redeem Israel. And what is more, it is the third day since all this took place. In addition, some of our women amazed us. They went to the tomb early this morning but didn't find his body. They came and told us that they had seen a vision of angels, who said he was alive. Then some of our companions went to the tomb and found it just as the women had said, but they did not see Jesus."

—Luke 24:19-24, NIV

These men saw Jesus as a mighty prophet but not as their Savior. And what was Christ's response? First, He told the men they were foolish and slow to believe all that the prophets had said. Without hesitation, Jesus then began filling the gaps of their broken faith. He started with Moses and all the prophets, explaining all the scriptures concerning Himself (Luke 24:25-27). It's a good thing this walk to Emmaus was seven miles long. But consider the scene. These two men had the opportunity to walk with Christ in the flesh as He explained to them His Word.

Now consider your time. You have the same opportunity to walk with Christ as He explains His words to you. Do you recognize His presence as you discuss Him with others?

It isn't until we knock on His door, and sit with Him as He breaks bread, that we truly experience Him. As the men approached Emmaus, they urged Jesus to stay with them. They knocked, and Jesus opened the door. He agreed to stay. Later, while at the table with them, Jesus took bread, gave thanks, and then broke it and began to give it to the men. When Christ did this, the men's eyes opened, and they recognized Him (Luke 24:28-31). And just like us, they questioned why they hadn't recognized Him before.

Full of excitement, the men got up, and rushed back to Jerusalem. They told the eleven disciples that the Lord's resurrection was true! As they discussed all these things, Jesus appeared and stood among them. The men were frightened, thinking they saw a ghost.

He said to them, "Why are you troubled, and why do doubts rise in your minds? Look at my hands and my feet. It is I myself! Touch me and see; a ghost does not have flesh and bones, as you see I have."

—Luke 24:38-39, NIV

Amazingly, some of them still did not believe. So, Jesus asked the men for something to eat. He took a piece of fish they gave Him and ate it in their presence. What was Christ doing? He was fellowshipping with them. He took what the men had and used it for His glory and their good.

Then he opened their minds so they could understand the Scriptures.

—Luke 24:45, NIV

Jesus told the men that they were witnesses to all that had happened. They saw Jesus crucified, and they saw Him as their risen Savior. In addition, Christ told His followers that repentance and forgiveness of sins would be preached in His name to every nation. His disciples would take part in this great commission.

Today, you and I are also part of this mission. Through our experiences with Christ, we are witnesses to what He has done for us and to the truth of His Word. If we fail to knock on His door, we miss the opportunity for Him to open our eyes and our minds so that we can know Him better. And the less we understand, the younger our spirits remain.

In 2005, I read a book that changed my life and set me on a path to spiritual maturity. I was 22 years old and had been a Christian for 18 years already. Though I read the Bible, my faith was still young. At the time, Josh and I were living in Corpus Christi, Texas. I had a lot of time on my hands during the baseball season. We didn't yet have children, which left me with many hours of the day to fill. And let's be honest. How many times a week can one clean an apartment? Outside of my household duties, I often visited bookstores. Josh and I both loved getting coffee and going to bookstores. Something about the smell of books envelops a person when walking through the doors. Then there are the convenient, comfortable chairs sitting around that beckon people to sit and relax.

On one such visit, Josh and I were standing in the Christian section when a book's title caught his attention. It was called *Learn the Bible in 24 Hours*. He thought it looked neat, and I grabbed it out of curiosity. I was at a place in life where I wanted to understand the Bible better, and the thought of doing this in 24 hours was very appealing.

In the days that followed, God allowed me to see His Word through the lens of prophecy. As a result, I made connections with books in the Bible that I never had before. This encounter birthed in me a desire to know God better. After this experience, I never looked at His Word in the same way.

As iron sharpens iron, God uses the commitment of other believers to springboard our faith. In our search for Him, the Lord puts people in our path to help us along and stay the course. And when these windows of time spent with God occur, we must cherish every moment. Similarly, we need to make decisions in life that lead to a plate of solid food rather than a bottle of milk. The result is spiritual growth. A sturdy faith that doesn't crush under the weight of earthly life.

We have life because Jesus came as a light to dispel the darkness (Genesis 1:3). In Christ is life, and that life has brought light to everyone (John 1:4). Not only does Jesus banish darkness, He releases eternal life to all who believe in Him. We've learned that those who walk in darkness do not know where they are going. But we, God's children, do know the way. The Lord makes it clear in His Word that we are to enter through the narrow gate.

"You can enter God's Kingdom only through the narrow gate. The highway to hell is broad, and its gate is wide for the many who choose that way. But the gateway to life is very narrow and the road is difficult, and only a few find it."
—Matthew 7:13-14, NLT

Only a few find the road that leads to life because many people do not believe in Christ. They remain in darkness when they could be walking down a brightly lit path paved for them by the shedding of Jesus' blood. As Christians, then, darkness is not an option. We've already made a choice to walk in the light, as Christ is in the light, so we can fellowship with one another (1 John 1:7).

Let us then put our lamps on a stand. For whatever is hidden is meant to be brought out into the open (Mark 4:22). Personal insights from God need to be made known to preserve our lives and to save the lives of our hearers (1 Timothy 4:16).

Again, Christ calls us to knock, and the door will be opened. As we dine with Him at His table, He fills us with His Word. And to whoever has, more will be given (Mark 4:25). The fullness of the Lord's wisdom and knowledge will prevent us from destruction. May we recline at the table, believing in His goodness, and trusting in His ways. For Jesus satisfies those who are thirsty and fills those who are hungry with good things (Psalm 107:9).

A Prayer for Your Journey:

Lord, may I not seek you without ever resting in your presence. I long for frequent visits at your table, enjoying solid food as we fellowship together. Help me to stay the course and to let my light shine because I do believe you are good. In Jesus' name, I pray, Amen.

A Hymn to Ponder:

Word of God Speak[16]

Song by: MercyMe

I'm finding myself at a loss for words
And the funny thing is it's okay
The last thing I need is to be heard
But to hear what You would say

Word of God speak
Would You pour down like rain
Washing my eyes to see
Your majesty
To be still and know
That You're in this place
Please let me stay and rest
In Your holiness
Word of God speak

I'm finding myself in the midst of You
Beyond the music, beyond the noise
All that I need is to be with You
And in the quiet hear Your voice

Word of God speak

---

16 "Word of God Speak - MercyMe." 2007. www.youtube.com. January 15, 2007. https://www.youtube.com/watch?v=4JK_6osCH74.

Would You pour down like rain
Washing my eyes to see
Your majesty
To be still and know
That You're in this place
Please let me stay and rest
In Your holiness

Word of God speak
Would You pour down like rain
Washing my eyes to see
Your majesty
To be still and know
That You're in this place
Please let me stay and rest
In Your holiness

I'm finding myself at a loss for words
And the funny thing is it's okay

Chapter 10

Piercing the Dark

When Josh played baseball at Eastern Kentucky University, he had an "old school" coach named Coach Ward. His four primary rules were: always polish your cleats, shave your face, know the quote of the day, and never be late. Luckily, Josh only broke two of the four as a young freshman.

From the time Josh was in elementary school, he was used to his mom waking him up with a hot cup of coffee. Like many families, sometimes they made it to school on time, and sometimes they didn't. However, as he transitioned to college, his newfound freedom forced him to learn additional responsibilities such as getting up on time. One morning he woke up startled at the view from his college dorm window. What he saw sent his heart racing because stretched out across the running track were his teammates. Every baseball player, except him, was preparing for conditioning. He had overslept. What was the consequence of his absence? Coach Ward told him to meet him at 6 am on the basketball court. As Josh ran suicides, Coach Ward enjoyed a hot cup of coffee.

Another rule Josh broke occurred when the afternoon sunlight danced across the baseball field. During practice, Coach Ward caught sight of something he disapproved of, which prompted him to question Josh about what he had growing on his face. As a young 18-year-old, Josh wasn't accustomed to shaving simply because he rarely had to. So, the question Coach Ward asked him caught him off guard. Josh said that his peach fuzz must have been glistening in the sunlight at the exact moment Coach Ward looked at him. What was the consequence? Once again, Josh met Coach Ward at 6 am.

Thankfully he kept his cleats polished, and he always knew the day's quote that Coach Ward wrote on the board in the locker room. I'd like to say that Josh's forgetfulness ended his first year of college, but that boat continued sailing into adulthood.

While living in Corpus Christi, Texas, Josh and I were filling the back of our car with groceries when he did something that even I couldn't believe. After we put up the last of the groceries, we headed down the highway back to our apartment. When I got out and went around the back to start unloading, something on the bumper took my breath. There, on the corner, sat Josh's wallet. His wallet literally rode on the bumper of our Tahoe, going sixty-plus miles an hour down a busy highway. And it didn't fall off. When Josh saw it, he first looked at me, and then when he thought he was in the clear, he said, "Can you believe my wallet didn't fall off?" I was less than enthused and responded with, "Can you believe you left your wallet *on* the bumper?"

All jokes aside, who of us hasn't forgotten something at some point? We can forget things even when we know the rules or expectations. The same principle applies to our Christian walks. The question is, what do we do with the words God gives us as we fellowship with Him? It's possible for us to spend time with the Lord and then forget what He tells us. This is especially true when our minds cloud with other worries, pressures, or stress. Then, in the heat of a difficult moment, we may act as if we never spent time with God or that we never received a Word from Him regarding our situations.

The danger in forgetting what the Lord tells us is that it can tempt us to put our hope in something else.

In a previous chapter, we talked about how the Israelites forgot the Lord while in the desert. They went so far as to make a golden image to worship. Their impatience led to their sin. You may be thinking that you would never do something that extreme, but our idols don't always come in the form of golden images. Anything we worship other than God is an idol. And if we've broken one of God's commandments, we've broken them all (James 2:10). I've struggled with this fact, even convincing myself that I haven't broken all of God's laws. But over time, the Holy Spirit has revealed truth to me regarding sin and the need for salvation.

In the book of Hosea, God says that the vilest form of adultery is departing from Him (Hosea 1:2). When we turn to the world for answers, after the Lord has already spoken to us, then we are departing from Him. We might need to take a moment to consider this. A spirit of prostitution can lead us astray, causing us to be unfaithful to God (Hosea 3:12).

Satan's goal for all Christians is to flee from the Lord. And when we are unfaithful to God, we become faithful to the enemy.

Still yet, if we haven't forgotten the Lord's words to us, there are times that we may shrink back from the knowledge we've acquired. And when we shrink back, we develop bad habits. For example, there was a period in Josh's baseball career when he felt pressured to change how he hit a baseball. Josh was always known for his speed, and as a lead-off hitter, his mission was always to get on base. If he could get to first, it wouldn't be long before he would be standing on second. Hitting home runs, then, was a bonus. But they were never his goal until he felt pressured to hit for more power.

When sports analysts characterized Josh as a player, their negative remarks circled around a belief that he lacked the ability to hit home runs. Over time this became a concern for Josh. But the more he focused on hitting for power, the more he developed bad habits when he swung a bat. I couldn't tell a difference in his swing from the sidelines. He would often ask me while he swung a bat in our apartment if I could see changes, and I know my blank stares weren't encouraging. Each new swing pattern brought him excitement, and I wanted to share in his optimism but struggled to see the benefit in a minor tweak.

Often redundancy causes us to miss important shifts. So as bad habits form in our spiritual lives, it's natural for us to normalize them. Before we realize it, our habits become part of our daily routines. We may say things like, "This is just the way I am," or "I can't help how God made me." But justifying subtle changes in our actions dismisses the need for correction. God didn't create us to have bitter attitudes in life or to live in a state of perpetual disappointment.

It's frustrating when we seek answers from others and come up short-handed. To the world, the things of God are considered foolishness (1 Corinthians 2:14). For us to correct bad habits and remember the Lord's words, we must return to the source of our hope.

But my righteous one will live by faith. And I take no pleasure in the one who shrinks back. But we do not belong to those who shrink back and are destroyed, but to those who have faith and are saved.
—Hebrews 10:38-39, NIV

If we are believers in Christ, then we must live by our faith. We have no other option. Even when we can't physically see the Lord's promises, we still believe what He tells us. Shrinking back from our faith not only displeases God but also leads to our destruction. Believing what He says saves us.

What happens when we don't forget the Lord's words or shrink back from them, but we just plain doubt them? One of the most significant tests of our faith comes when we've received a Word from God, and then our circumstances abruptly change, causing His words to appear contradictory. As previously described, the Lord told me that my faith had healed me (Matthew 9:22) before I knew I had breast cancer. Upon receiving His Word, I was only aware of the lump I had, but not its severity. When God told me that He healed me, I never once thought I had cancer. Honestly, I mentally dismissed the notion. So, you can imagine my reaction when my doctor called me with the news. Her words were the exact opposite of what the Lord told me. How could I have cancer if God healed me?

When we receive a Word from the Lord, we have a choice to make: we can believe what He says or not believe.

Underline this: the devil will immediately ignite doubt in the life of believers after they have heard from the Lord. This habit of his started with the beginning of God's creation. After creating Adam and Eve, the Lord told them they could eat from any tree in the Garden of Eden except the tree of knowledge of good and evil. If they ate from this tree, they would die. And what did Satan say after God gave these instructions?

Now the serpent was more crafty than any of the wild animals the Lord God had made. He said to the woman, "Did God really say, 'You must not eat from any tree in the garden'?"
—Genesis 3:1, NIV

Notice how Satan twisted God's words in his attempt to spark doubt in Eve. God didn't say they couldn't eat from any tree in the garden. Only one was forbidden. But this question prompted Eve to give the enemy her attention.

The woman said to the serpent, "We may eat fruit from the trees in the garden, but God did say, 'You must not eat fruit from the tree that is in the middle of the garden, and you must not touch it, or you will die.'"
—Genesis 3:2-3, NIV

Satan never mentioned the tree in the middle of the garden when he approached Eve. She did. The enemy got Eve to open up and talk and then he used her words to lie.

"You will not certainly die," the serpent said to the woman. "For God knows that when you eat from it your eyes will be opened, and you will be like God, knowing good and evil."
—Genesis 3:4-5, NIV

Didn't Satan want to be God? We all know where his corruption landed him. He was banished from heaven itself (Ezekiel 28:17), and there he was in the garden using the same tactic with Eve. He first caused Eve to doubt, and then he lied to her. Sadly, Eve believed him. If she ate from this tree, she would be like God in one way--knowing good and evil. But she most certainly would face death. After tasting the fruit, her and Adam's life changed on Earth, ushering sin into the world. Satan's ability to win the battle with Adam and Eve still affects us today.

He uses the same scheme with us. The enemy puts the exact phrase into our heads as he did with Eve, "Did God really say…?" And we, as believers, must use God's words to overcome his lies. Think of what the cost is by not believing what God tells you. Doubting the Lord will not only affect your life, but it will affect the lives of those around you.

Not believing what the Lord tells us also means we don't have faith. And without faith, it's impossible to please God (Hebrews 11:6). So, what must we do with God's Word? First, we need to stand on what He tells us, refusing to believe anything else. We can do this by storing God's Word in our hearts.

I have hidden your word in my heart that I might not sin against you.
—Psalm 119:11, NIV

Hiding God's Word in our hearts means that we can recall it. Not only will we remember what the Lord tells us, but the act of hiding His words prevents us from sinning against Him. This is why it's important to know the condition of your heart. If your heart is calloused, the act of recalling God's Word is extremely difficult.

When God told me that my faith healed me, I chose to believe Him. Believing Him keeps me from being unfaithful to Him. And after we store God's Word in our hearts, we must guard them for safekeeping.

Guard your heart above all else, for it determines the course of your life.
—Proverbs 4:23, NLT

When we store God's Word without guarding our hearts, we're in danger of the enemy stealing the truth we've obtained. It's like seed sown along the path readily available for the enemy to grab. By giving Satan an open door to snatch God's Word, he has a real chance of destroying us. The course of our lives will then derail, causing us to fall further and further away from the path God designed for us to travel. Ultimately, we will miss accomplishing our true purpose in life. The good news is that God helps us protect our hearts.

Don't worry about anything; instead, pray about everything. Tell God what you need, and thank him for all he has done. Then you will experience God's peace, which exceeds anything we can understand. His peace will guard your hearts and minds as you live in Christ Jesus.
—Philippians 4:6-7, NLT

<u>Instructions from Philippians 4:6-7:</u>

1. Don't worry about anything
2. Pray about everything
3. Tell God what you need
4. Thank Him for all He has done

<u>What we will experience:</u>

God's peace

Our hearts are protected when we have peace from God. Think of peace as a wall of defense against the enemy. The more peace we have, the less chance Satan has of breaking through and stealing God's Word.

We receive this peace through obedience. After casting our worries aside, the Lord tells us to pray about everything. I don't know about you, but my prayer life hasn't always been what it should be. I have fallen into the trap of not praying at times, because I've told myself that God is all-knowing and already has a plan. Since God knows what will happen, what's the point in praying about everything? Unfortunately, this attitude can prevent us from exercising our faith. Prayer is the single most powerful tool Christians have to communicate with God. As Jesus breathed His final breath, the temple's curtain tore in two (Luke 23:45). This act grants all believers access to the very throne of God. If we halt our prayers, we are shutting off correspondence with the Lord and losing hope of having any peace.

What happens when God's response is different from our prayers? Often frustration or sadness sets in when our prayers do not pan out the way we hoped they would. In such fragile moments, we must be careful of our reactions to the movement of God's hand. He answers our prayers according to our faith (Matthew 9:29), aligned with His will (1 John 5:14).

Satan wants us to believe that God doesn't answer our prayers because we lack faith. This isn't always the case. I've prayed for the healing of others, believing in God's healing power, without seeing Him perform the miracle I expected. But guarding my heart prevents me from turning my back on the Lord. Again, God's peace that surpasses our earthly thinking is what protects our hearts and averts our destruction. For example, we will see some people we pray for healed before our very eyes on Earth, and others we will see healed when we get to heaven. The point to grasp is that if we stop praying, we will cease all hope of having peace and experiencing any miracles. Jesus tells us that He doesn't give to us as the world does. Peace is a gift that can only come from Him. Our hearts shouldn't be troubled or afraid (John 14:27).

Before being arrested, Jesus Himself prayed to the Father. Unlike us, He knew the outcome before He ever prayed. Regardless of His awareness, however, Christ still exercised His faith.

"Father, if you are willing, take this cup from me; yet not my will, but yours be done."

—Luke 22:42, NIV

After praying, an angel came and strengthened the Lord. But the outcome of His impending death didn't change. The Father didn't remove Christ's cup. Does this mean Christ didn't have faith? Certainly not. He desired the Father's will above His own. And His commitment pierced the darkness.

Just as Christ came to Earth to destroy Satan's work (1 John 3:8), we who believe in Jesus can also extinguish the enemy's plans. When Satan tempts us to sin or be unfaithful to the Lord, Jesus provides us a way out so that we can survive such enticements (1 Corinthians 10:13). And each time we stand on God's Word, believing what He's told us, we also pierce the darkness. Our resistance to the enemy causes him to flee from us (James 4:7).

If we have protected God's Word in our hearts, we can readily recall what we've learned. Let's practice writing down what the Lord tells us and saying it aloud. This way, we can always be ready to give a reason for our hope (1 Peter 3:15).

When I initially learned that I had breast cancer, I told my family that I was standing on God's promise of healing. On social media, I shared Matthew 9:22 (NIV), which again states, *"Take heart, daughter," he said. "your faith has healed you."* My youngest sister had a bracelet made with that verse on it without me knowing. She desired that I wear it while getting my chemotherapy treatments to remember God's Word. I took her wants a step further because I wear the bracelet nearly every day. I don't just want to remember what the Lord told me when I get treatments. I want to remember His words while sitting on the couch, doing laundry, washing the dishes, and helping my kids with their homework. I don't ever want to forget God's promise to me, because if I forget, then I'm in danger of doubting.

The bracelet is a constant reminder of God's faithfulness. It also allows me to readily explain my hope because each time I look down at my wrist, I see Matthew 9:22. I don't have to fumble for words when God's Word is right in front of me and stored in my heart.

And this Word needs to be shared with others. Earlier I stated that doubting the Lord will affect the lives of those around us. In my situation, if I lack faith in what God has told me, how will that affect my husband and children? What will their response be when others inquire of my well-being? Often our emotional state is readily observed. People can read how we are faring by our expressions. If worry and anxiety fill my home, do you think my family will show these emotions in public? There is an increased chance that others will sense the very cares that God tells us to cast on Him

(1 Peter 5:7). The stability of my home depends directly on my acceptance of God's Word.

In the same way, let your light shine before others, that they may see your good deeds and glorify your Father in heaven.
—Matthew 5:16, NIV

Shining our light isn't solely for our good but the good of others. When other people see us exercise our faith on mountaintops and in the valleys, they will praise the Lord. And in turn, their light will shine.

No matter how tough life gets or what we've lost due to following Christ, our goal is to stay the course until we breathe our last. During Jesus' earthly ministry, there was a time when He was warned to get out of Jerusalem. A group of Pharisees told Him to leave and go somewhere else because Herod wanted to kill Him. If issued a death threat, some of us may be tempted to flee. But not Jesus. His response to the Pharisees showed His unwillingness to dodge His calling.

He replied, "Go tell that fox, 'I will keep on driving out demons and healing people today and tomorrow, and on the third day I will reach my goal.' In any case, I must press on today and tomorrow and the next day – for surely no prophet can die outside Jerusalem!"
—Luke 13:32-33, NIV

Jesus had to keep going and so do we. He didn't turn to the right or the left of His mission. Nothing or no one was going to thwart His plans, and because of His commitment to follow through, He was able to say, *"It is finished,"* as He breathed His final breath (John 19:30).

Following Christ's example, we need to make every effort to enter through the narrow door. And once we've entered, our goal is to remain faithful as He is faithful. Jesus is the groom, and we, His church, are the bride (Revelation 19:7). The Lord uses a covenant we are familiar with to describe the intimacy He shares with us. On Earth, when man and woman join in Christian marriage, their promise to remain faithful is not only to one another but also to Christ.

On my wedding day, shades of plum, violet, and white filled the sanctuary of my home church. I remember taking my stepfather's arm and standing in front of two large double doors as tears filled my eyes. When the doors opened to the sanctuary with many guests, they each rose to their feet, and I wondered if I was feeling anything like a princess. Symmetrical white columns graced the platform. Hanging along the arch and cascading downward were layers of artificial vines and flowers that Josh's mom borrowed from her church. Peeking from behind these florals were white icicle lights we cleverly taped up along the back of the columns.

In front of this lovely backdrop stood my husband-to-be. Wearing a black tuxedo, he stood waiting for his bride. And at the end of that long aisle, I saw the boy I fell in love with. He was the one God picked for me, and I continued towards him, stepping through white rose petals. That day Josh and I promised each other and God that we would love one another until death we would part.

And God is waiting for His bride, the church. When we become a part of His family, we promise Him our love and devotion until death we meet. What a glorious day it will be when our Jesus we will see!

Therefore what God has joined together, let no one separate.
—Mark 10:9, NIV

This verse is true of husbands and wives but also the church with Christ. May no one separate what we have with the Lord. Early in our relationships with Him, we have much to discover and learn. The connection is tender without firm roots. But as we stay committed to Him, depending on Him for our every need, He fills us with His knowledge and wisdom. And in turn, we know Him better.

If we can commit our lives to another through earthly marriage without knowing what the future holds, how much more so should we commit ourselves to our heavenly Father? Our relationships with Him are eternal, and His nature is one we never have to question. There are no surprises with the Lord because He is the same yesterday, today, and forever (Hebrews 13:8).

Those who turn from Him give up the grace that could be theirs (Jonah 2:8). Unfortunately, Jonah learned this lesson the hard way. After running away from God, he nearly lost his life by being tossed overboard into the depths of the sea. But God had mercy on him and provided time for Jonah to realize the seriousness of His Word. Jonah spent three days and nights inside a great fish. While inside the fish, Jonah prayed these words.

"I cried out to the Lord in my great trouble, and he answered me.
I called to you from the land of the dead, and Lord, you heard me!
You threw me into the ocean depths, and I sank down to the heart of the sea.
The mighty waters engulfed me;
I was buried beneath your wild and stormy waves.
Then I said, 'O Lord, you have driven me from your presence.
Yet I will look once more toward your holy Temple.'
I sank beneath the waves, and the waters closed over me.
Seaweed wrapped itself around my head.
I sank down to the very roots of the mountains.
I was imprisoned in the earth, whose gates lock shut forever.
But you, O Lord my God, snatched me from the jaws of death!
As my life was slipping away, I remembered the Lord.
And my earnest prayer went out to you in your holy Temple.
Those who worship false gods turn their backs on all God's mercies.
But I will offer sacrifices to you with songs of praise,
and I will fulfill all my vows.
For my salvation comes from the Lord alone."

—Jonah 2:1-9, NLT

While in peril, Jonah remembered the saving grace of God. He knew the Lord saved his life and understood that disobedience leads to one's ruin. Six words show Jonah's renewed commitment: *"I will fulfill all my vows"* (Jonah 2:9). When he spoke those words, God gave Jonah a fresh start, allowing him to continue his mission.

I pray that we never forget, shrink back, or doubt God's Words to us. Believing what He tells us preserves our lives, allowing us to run our race with confidence. And the Lord's peace that surpasses our understanding will guard our hearts as we go the distance.

Your faithfulness to the Lord shatters the darkness of the enemy. God sees your devotion to Him, and He knows you by name (Isaiah 43:1). Great is your reward!

A Prayer for Your Journey:

Lord, I am so thankful for my relationship with you. Your Word is truth, and I pray you will help me to never forget that. I stand on your Word, Lord, knowing that departing from it will destroy me. Even when life gets tough, I vow to make good my commitment to you. In Jesus' name, I pray, Amen.

A Hymn to Ponder:

Great is Thy Faithfulness[17]

Written By: Thomas O. Chisholm
Song By: Carrie Underwood & CeCe Winans

"Great is Thy faithfulness," O God my Father,
There is no shadow of turning with Thee;
Thou changest not, Thy compassions, they fail not
As Thou hast been Thou forever wilt be.

"Great is Thy faithfulness!" "Great is Thy faithfulness!"
Morning by morning new mercies I see;
All I have needed Thy hand hath provided –
"Great is Thy faithfulness," Lord, unto me!

Summer and winter, springtime and harvest,
Sun, moon and stars in their courses above,
Join with all nature in manifold witness
To Thy great faithfulness, mercy and love.

"Great is Thy faithfulness!" "Great is Thy faithfulness!"
Morning by morning new mercies I see;
All I have needed Thy hand hath provided –

[17] "Carrie Underwood - Great Is Thy Faithfulness Ft. CeCe Winans (Official Performance Video)." 2021. www.youtube.com. April 5, 2021. https://www.youtube.com/watch?v=NT0HcAr9aeI.

"Great is Thy faithfulness," Lord, unto me!

Pardon for sin and a peace that endureth,
Thine own dear presence to cheer and to guide;
Strength for today and bright hope for tomorrow,
Blessings all mine, with ten thousand beside!

"Great is Thy faithfulness!" "Great is Thy faithfulness!"
Morning by morning new mercies I see;
All I have needed Thy hand hath provided –
"Great is Thy faithfulness,"
"Great is Thy faithfulness,"
"Great is Thy faithfulness,"
Lord, unto me!

Chapter 11

Bright Lights Up Ahead

In 2011, one year after Josh played in his last professional baseball game, the Lord called me to a significant task. It was July 15th, and I was on my way to get my hair done. At that point, the only time I had to myself was when I was in the car alone. My son was nearing two years old, and my daughter was almost one. Taking care of them required 24/7 attention. So, during the twenty-minute drive, I started talking to God about my life. In particular, I pondered my life with Josh. I didn't understand what his baseball career meant or why it ended the way it did when the Lord prompted me to write our story down. And with little awareness of my calling, I told Him I would.

Initially, I radiated with excitement because I was writing a book. Who could have ever imagined me doing something like that? I was so enthused that I immediately told my family the book would be finished within six months. Now, let's all pause for a short laugh! But I originally wasn't laughing because I was determined to complete this task. In the beginning, that's exactly what this calling was for me. I wanted to finish the assignment for God and check it off my to-do list. How hard could it be to write about a small-town boy making it to the big leagues?

Um, much harder than I thought. For years I tried to remember important details that weren't really important to develop chapters to a book that wasn't going anywhere. It was like running a marathon while carrying a thousand marbles. Words slipped here and fell there clouding any possibility of a real finish line. I couldn't grasp the pages that seemed to have no point. During this time, I questioned my purpose and gave God many reasons why I shouldn't write.

It turns out that writing about baseball life isn't what God wanted me to do. I spent nine years illuminating my and Josh's life when all along God was supposed to be the hero. What changed my direction? In September 2020, my friend sent me an application to Lysa Terkeurst's Book Proposal Bootcamp. The camp aims to teach writers how to organize and complete a professional book proposal. As I read the application, I noticed one major hurdle typed in bold at the bottom of the page: No Memoirs Accepted.

How could I fill out the application if I couldn't write a memoir? Despite the obstacle, I told my friend that I would still try to answer the questions. As I typed my last response, I scrolled to the top of the page and reread my answers. Tears filled my eyes as God revealed the beginnings of a book I had never considered. In those moments, the Lord opened my eyes to the actual story I was supposed to share. And I was selected as one of 100 participants for the Spring 2021 Book Proposal Bootcamp to begin the process.

I never finished the memoir about Josh and me because it wasn't the right message. Now looking back at the footprints of our marriage I see God's healing power rather than Josh's accomplishments. We both needed to die to ourselves so that we could share in Christ's sufferings. It was not until we experienced this that we could help anyone else. I told the Lord I wished I would have known earlier what He truly wanted me to write because it would have saved me a lot of time.

But He told me that His revelations await appointed times (Habakkuk 2:3) because His patience is my salvation (2 Peter 3:15).

The years I spent writing were not a waste of time. The Lord had much to teach me, and I needed time to gain His wisdom. As I near the end of this book, I do not regret a single moment I wrestled with God. Even the moments I begged Him to remove my calling because of the difficulty I had trying to accomplish it. He has shown me that His power is made perfect in my weaknesses (2 Corinthians 12:9).

What motivates us to continue our race when the going gets tough? We've learned that our commitment to God often brings hardship into our lives. When Josh and I initially obeyed the Lord and turned away from professional baseball, our devotion didn't automatically usher in green pastures. We struggled financially, questioned our purpose, felt inadequate, and had little joy. Our future was dark, and we couldn't see what God was doing. The unknown sabotaged our contentment.

Beneath our hurt, however, was a flicker of hope. Deep down, we still believed God was good and that He would make the next season of our lives clear. And this belief saved us. Over time, we saw purpose emerge from our experiences.

For us to journey on with God, we must renew our minds daily.

Don't copy the behavior and customs of this world, but let God transform you into a new person by changing the way you think. Then you will learn to know God's will for you, which is good, and pleasing, and perfect.
—Romans 12:2, NLT

God must change the way we think. He can only do this when we spend time with Him. Then, as our desires align with Him, the Lord reveals to us His will for our lives. This will is good, pleasing, and perfect. Do you know what this means? We can enjoy doing what it is God has called us to do. And that pleasure is reciprocated in Him.

No matter the journey, when we accomplish God's will, He is pleased (Hebrews 13:16).

What greater reward is there than putting a smile on the Father's face? Jesus Himself experienced this when He carried out the Father's will. After performing many miracles, Jesus took Peter, James, and John up on a high mountain. Christ then transfigured Himself, allowing the men to see His heavenly likeness. His face shone like the sun, and His clothes became as white as light. Moses and Elijah even appeared and began talking to Jesus (Matthew 17:1-3).

While he was still speaking, a bright cloud covered them, and a voice from the cloud said, "This is my Son, whom I love; with him I am well pleased. Listen to him!"
—Matthew 17:5, NIV

The voice scared Peter, James, and John as they bowed down in terror. But Jesus touched them and told them to get up and not be afraid. And the same message applies to us. We are to get up and not be afraid to carry out the Lord's plans for our lives. By doing so, we please Him, and in turn, ourselves are pleased. We can start enjoying our lives and experiencing contentment when we agree that God's plan is best.

A single encounter with the Lord can transition us from darkness to light or confusion to understanding. Paul went from persecuting Christians to being persecuted for becoming a Christian. He threw off his former life to take hold of that which is eternal - a relationship with Jesus. And what caused this change? An encounter with Christ on the road to Damascus. Jonah went from fleeing God to returning to Him. He learned the importance of God's Word and what it means to agree with Him. And what caused this change? Spending three days and nights in the belly of a great fish.

We may not all get stopped in the middle of the road or get swallowed by a great fish, but we will all have a moment with the Lord that requires us to make a decision. Many of you reading this book have already agreed to the Lord's calling. You may have lost your dream by walking away from a career, losing a relationship you loved, or leaving a church family you valued to do ministry elsewhere. Some of you have even packed up your things and left your home to go after what Christ has called you to. These actions have enabled you to become doers of the Word and not just hearers.

So do not throw away your confidence; it will be richly rewarded. You need to persevere so that when you have done the will of God, you will receive what he has promised. For, "In just a little while, he who is coming will come and will not delay."

—Hebrews 10:35-37, NIV

What has God promised those who do His will? He's promised us eternal life. We don't need to fear dying a physical death because we, who are faithful, will not endure a spiritual death. Let us look forward to the day when the Lord says, *"Well done, my good and faithful servant"* (Matthew 25:21, NLT). Christ is coming, and His return will not delay, so we must be ready at all times to meet Him.

The decisions we make on Earth determine our readiness to meet the Lord.

After watching a fellow believer use this analogy, Josh considered the importance of the comparison. He began using the following object lesson to put our time on Earth versus eternity into perspective. While speaking to a group of teenagers, Josh took a 100-foot white rope and wrapped it around the area where he stood. Josh then held up the first couple of inches of the rope he had wrapped black tape around and told the teens to look at the small black section representing their time on Earth. He said the decisions we make during this short span determine where we spend eternity. The rest of the rope is one of two places: heaven or hell. And even the rope couldn't do eternity justice because, in reality, eternity never ends. But as gazing eyes drifted from the black tape to the rest of the rope, hearts began to change.

Our lives are but a vapor that appears for a time and then vanishes (James 4:14). Therefore, conforming to the world is a waste of our time. We need to pack light because we are simply passing through. There are no reasons to hold firm to a temporary life. Earthly accolades will not distinguish us from one another in heaven. We will be known for our faith in Christ and what we did with that faith.

Presently, our job is to show mercy to those who doubt, save others from the fire, and show grace with fear, hating even clothing stained from corrupted flesh (Jude 1:22-23). To hate clothing stained from corrupted flesh is to hate sin and association with it. Sin separates us from God (Isaiah 59:2), and when we tolerate it, we conform to the world. People who abandon Christ's teaching are grumblers and faultfinders, following their evil desires (Jude 1:16). They create division among believers and do not have the Spirit (Jude 1:19).

Those who live according to the flesh have their minds set on what the flesh desires; but those who live in accordance with the Spirit have their minds set on what the Spirit desires. The mind governed by the flesh is death, but the mind governed by the Spirit is life and peace.

—Romans 8:5-6, NIV

For the Spirit to control our minds, we must renew them every single day.

While wrapped in flesh, there is no other way for us to stay on track with God's will. Paul even speaks of the war that rages against the mind and body. He says that what he does is not the good he wants to do (Romans 7:19). I think we've all been there. We have days where we follow the Spirit's guidance and have peace. Then there are times that we let sin take over and have its way of bringing about our destruction. The good news is that if the Spirit of God lives in us, then we are not controlled by our sinful natures (Romans 8:9). Through Christ, we can receive forgiveness of our sins, restoring our union with Him.

Being obedient to Christ establishes a love relationship with Him. As we walk with Him, we begin to talk to Him, listen to His voice, and obey Him. Our minds start to fill with the things of God, and He becomes a part of our everyday lives. The space He takes up in our minds frees us from our sinful nature. Not that we will ever be perfect while on Earth, but we will become more and more like Christ the more time we spend with Him.

We have this promise that God saves those who stand firm to the end (Matthew 24:13). So, let's set our minds on things above, not on earthly things (Colossians 3:2). Eternity in heaven will be unlike anything we have ever imagined.

"Never again will they hunger; never again will they thirst. The sun will not beat down on them, nor any scorching heat. For the Lamb at the center of the throne will be their shepherd; he will lead them to springs of living water. And God will wipe away every tear from their eyes."

—Revelation 7:16-17, NIV

There is coming a day when we will never feel hunger, thirst, sadness, or hurt. This truth encourages us to persevere in our faith. We will see loved ones that we've lost and other believers we've never met. Fellowship with the Lord will never end, and we will remain in His presence forever. Even the description of heaven is worth pondering. So, let's pause and read about the beauty of our heavenly home:

It shone with the glory of God, and its brilliance was like that of a very precious jewel, like a jasper, clear as crystal. It had a great, high wall with twelve gates, and with twelve angels at the gates. On the gates were written the names of the twelve tribes of Israel. The wall of the city had twelve foundations, and on them were the names of the twelve apostles of the Lamb. The wall was made of jasper, and the city of pure gold, as pure as glass. The foundations of the city walls were decorated with every kind of precious stone. The first foundation was jasper, the second sapphire, the third agate, the fourth emerald, the fifth onyx, the sixth ruby, the seventh chrysolite, the eighth beryl, the ninth topaz, the tenth turquoise, the eleventh jacinth, and the twelfth amethyst. The twelve gates were twelve pearls, each gate made of a single pearl. The great street of the city was of gold, as pure as transparent glass.

—Revelation 21:11-12, 14, 18-21, NIV

Once, I researched each jewel that creates the wall around the new heavenly Jerusalem. I copied images and then stacked these images in order on a blank spreadsheet to get a better sense of what I was envisioning. Such depictions are awe-inspiring but still do not serve heaven justice because of the brilliancy of light that will be present. There will not be a need for the sun or the moon to shine there, because the glory of God is its light and the Lamb its lamp (Revelation 21:23). Therefore, life in this eternity will never experience darkness.

But is the promise of our heavenly home enough to preserve our faith on Earth? Though drenched in beauty, in the presence of God, sometimes heaven seems distant. Like a faraway land that we've heard about while simultaneously forgetting it's real. However, heaven is only obscured in our minds if we cast it aside. That's why we must keep our focus on things above so the promise of eternity with Christ is never forgotten.

Doing God's will for our lives is the best way to keep our focus on Him and on our heavenly home. Even if this commitment is lonely, God's promises are still valid. The description of heaven we read above was written down in Revelation by John, the apostle. He endured suffering as a prisoner on the island of Patmos for spreading the word about Jesus.[18] While on the island, he received a vision that Jesus revealed to him. Revelation is the only book in the Bible that promises a blessing to those who read the words of the prophecy, hear it, and take it to heart (Revelation 1:3). We must consider what is in store for us as believers and nonbelievers. For the time of these events is near.

The word "near" may very well mean within our lifetimes. Jesus is returning, and He won't delay. Nothing will hinder the words of Revelation from occurring because God isn't a liar (Hebrews 6:18). That's why we must always be ready regardless of what our calling involves.

Being prepared to meet the Lord face-to-face requires our immediate focus on Earth.

Have you ever gotten distracted by fellow believers and wondered why their lives appear more manageable than yours? Truthfully, we never know what the lives of others are like. Some people stay positive, masking their

---

[18] Alexander, David, and Pat Alexander. 1999. *Zondervan Handbook to the Bible.* Grand Rapids, Mi Zondervan Pub. House.

hurts, while others show them more freely. Therefore, we can't compare ourselves to others while questioning God's sovereignty.

After Jesus' resurrection, He appeared to His disciples by the sea of Tiberias. They were fishing as Jesus stood on the shore and called out to them. First, He asked the men if they had any fish. After they said no, Jesus instructed them to throw their nets on the other side of the boat and when they did, they could barely handle the net because of the large number of fish they caught. While He spoke to them, John realized that Jesus was standing on the shore, and when he exclaimed the news, Peter grabbed his outer garment and jumped into the water (John 21:1-7).

Peter's journey with God had its share of ups and downs. Peter loved the Lord, but he was impulsive, made mistakes, deserted God, and even denied Him. But despite Peter's past, his purpose remained. God had a plan for Peter and made this plan known to him.

When they had finished eating, Jesus said to Simon Peter, "Simon son of John, do you love me more than these?"
"Yes, Lord," he said, "you know that I love you."
Jesus said, "Feed my lambs."
Again Jesus said, "Simon son of John, do you love me?"
He answered, "Yes, Lord, you know that I love you."
Jesus said, "Take care of my sheep."
The third time he said to him, "Simon son of John, do you love me?"
Peter was hurt because Jesus asked him the third time, "Do you love me?" He said, "Lord, you know all things; you know that I love you."
Jesus said, "Feed my sheep."
—John 21:15-17, NIV

I often wonder if Jesus asked Peter this question three times because that's the same number of times Peter previously denied Him. Indeed, Christ knew Peter's heart was full of love for Him, but He allowed Peter to express his devotion. After this, Jesus told Peter that when he is old, he will stretch out his hands for someone else to dress him and lead him where he doesn't want to go. Jesus tells him this to indicate the kind of death Peter would endure--one that would glorify God (John 21:18-19).

Right after Peter hears these words, Jesus says to him, *"Follow me!"* (John 21:19). To put the verses into perspective, first, Jesus confirms Peter's love for Him, then indicates the type of death Peter would endure, and finally, He instructs Peter to follow Him. You see, the road we travel will not always be easy. Some of us will endure trials more difficult than others. But God's instruction to us is all the same. We are to follow Him every step of the way.

As Jesus gave His instructions to Peter, Peter noticed that another disciple was following them.

When Peter saw him, he asked, "Lord, what about him?"
—John 21:21, NIV

Here Jesus was in the middle of a meaningful discussion when Peter's eyes drifted away from Him. And without hesitation, Peter became more concerned about the fate of another disciple. He might as well have said, "Ok, Lord, I hear what you're telling me, but what about this guy over here?"

Again, have you ever questioned God about someone else? When we lose our dreams or hear life-altering news, it's tempting to ask if others will have the same destiny. Or we might wonder why others aren't required to experience the same hardships.

I previously mentioned that when Josh left the game of baseball, it was difficult for him to watch the sport on TV. The most painful reason for this struggle rested in the reality that his friends were still getting to live out their dreams. If Josh couldn't continue, then why were they allowed to? It's a logical question, but not one we are to be concerned with. That's exactly what God told Peter.

Jesus answered, "If I want him to remain alive until I return, what is that to you? You must follow me."
—John 21:22, NIV

We are not to get caught up in God's plans for others. That is His concern, not ours. Our job is to follow the Lord, no matter what that entails. When we focus on what others are doing, we lose sight of our mission. That's why God tells us to fix our gaze directly before us, making level paths for our feet and taking ways that are firm. We aren't to swerve to the right or left (Proverbs 4:25-27).

There is much in store for those who do God's will to the end. The Lord even has a name for us who accomplish this. We are called overcomers (Revelation 2:26). When Christ gave John the vision of

Revelation, He revealed seven promises to overcomers. I've attached Tim Lahaye's commentary to further explain each of these promises.[19]

1. *"The one who has an ear, let him hear what the Spirit says to the churches. To the one who overcomes, I will grant to eat from the tree of life, which is in the Paradise of God."* (Revelation 2:7, NASB) The tree of life is the one Adam and Eve were forbidden to eat after their sin. For those of us who put our trust in the Lord, this tree is a symbol of eternity in the paradise of God.

2. *"The one who has an ear, let him hear what the Spirit says to the churches. The one who overcomes will not be hurt by the second death."* (Revelation 2:11, NASB) God's children have Christ's promise that they will never be hurt by the second death - the lake of fire (Revelation 20:14). Death occurs when a person is forever separated from God instead of united with Him. Overcomers must not fear this death because it has no power over them.

3. *"The one who has an ear, let him hear what the Spirit says to the churches. To the one who overcomes, I will give some of the hidden manna, and I will give him a white stone, and a new name written on the stone which no one knows except the one who receives it."* (Revelation 2:17, NASB) Manna was the heavenly food sent by God to the children of Israel in the desert. Just as the Israelites had to go individually and gather their supply, so the child of God must depend on God for his or her individual spiritual supply. The white stone is a symbol of the eternal acquittal we acquire through faith in Jesus.

4. *"The one who overcomes, and the one who keeps My deeds until the end, I will give him authority over the nations – And he shall rule them with a rod of iron, as the vessels of the potter are shattered, as I also have received authority from My Father; and I will give him the morning star. The one who has an ear, let him hear what the Spirit says to the churches."* (Revelation 2:26-29, NASB) Christ will give overcomers a position of leadership and authority and also the morning star which is the promise of Christ Himself.

5. *"The one who overcomes will be clothed the same way, in white garments; and I will not erase his name from the book of life, and I will confess his name before my Father and before His angels. The one who has an ear, let him hear what*

[19] Lahaye, Tim. 1999. *Revelation Unveiled.* Grand Rapids, Mich.: Zondervan.

the Spirit says to the churches." (Revelation 3:5-6, NASB) Dressed in white refers to being clothed in the righteousness of Christ, and we who overcome have security. Our names will remain in the book of life.

6. *"The one who overcomes, I will make him a pillar in the temple of My God, and he will not go out from it anymore; and I will write on him the name of My God, and the name of the city of My God, the new Jerusalem, which comes down out of heaven from My God, and My new name. The one who has an ear, let him hear what the Spirit says to the churches."* (Revelation 3:12-13, NASB) Pillars speak of stability, which all overcomers will have. True believers are identified with Christ by the seal of the name of God, which permits them to have entrance into the city of God.
7. *"The one who overcomes, I will grant to him to sit with Me on My throne, as I also overcame and sat down with My Father on His throne. The one who has an ear, let him hear what the Spirit says to the churches."* (Revelation 3:21-22, NASB) Overcomers will rule and reign with Christ in His coming kingdom.

Notice that each promise either begins or ends with a common audience. To those with ears, let us hear what the Spirit is telling us. This reference isn't describing physical ears but spiritual ones in tune with the voice of God. We who overcome this world, by believing Jesus is the Son of God (1 John 5:5), have much to look forward to! And these promises are eternal.

"Look, I am coming soon! My reward is with me, and I will give to each person according to what they have done. I am the Alpha and the Omega, the First and the Last, the Beginning and the End. Blessed are those who wash their robes, that they may have the right to the tree of life and may go through the gates into the city. Outside are the dogs, those who practice magic arts, the sexually immoral, the murderers, the idolaters and everyone who loves and practices falsehood. I, Jesus, have sent my angel to give you this testimony for the churches. I am the Root and the Offspring of David, and the bright Morning Star."

—Revelation 22:12-16, NIV

May these words be an encouragement to you as you continue your journey! To live is Christ, and to die is gain (Philippians 1:21). Therefore, while we are living, let us continue in the teaching of our Savior so that we can overcome that which threatens to hinder us.

A Prayer for Your Journey:

Lord, as I shift my focus on you, I am made more aware of your saving grace. May I not become lukewarm, losing my dependence on you, but eager to accomplish your will for my life. When I consider your sacrifice for me and what you have prepared for those who love you, I am in awe of you. In Jesus' name, I pray, Amen.

A Hymn to Ponder:

Rejoice[20]

Song By: Andrew Ripp

Until I rise like the morning
Wake up in the arms of glory
To finally see the sun
Above the pouring rain

Until I fall into surrenders
Healing hands and remember
There's a river on the other side of pain

I'm gonna
Rejoice, rejoice
Lift it up in the highs and lows
There's a better day coming
I know

Rejoice, rejoice
I'm gonna sing either way it goes
There's a better day coming
I know, I know

[20] "Andrew Ripp - Rejoice (Official Lyric Video)." 2021. www.youtube.com. April 21, 2021. https://www.youtube.com/watch?v=O5GFOD1TerU.

I know, I know

Until the boundary lines have broken
The levy gives and hearts spill open
To flood the land we fight over with endless love

Until forgiveness steals the blame
Of every heart, soul, mind, and strength
Until we know there's nothing left to do but trust
Oh, I'm gonna

Rejoice, rejoice
Lift it up in the highs and lows
There's a better day coming
I know

Rejoice, rejoice
I'm gonna sing either way it goes
There's a better day coming
I know, I know

(There's a better day coming) I know, I know
(There's a better day coming) I know, I know

Oh, my soul, send in the choir
Raise my song in the flood or the fire
Oh, my soul, send in the choir
Hope is ringing out higher and higher
Oh, my soul, send in the choir
Raise my song in the flood or the fire
Oh, my soul, send in the choir
Hope is ringing out higher and higher

Rejoice, and again I say, rejoice
Lift it up in the highs and lows
There's a better day coming, I know

Rejoice (rejoice)
I'm gonna sing it either way it goes (Yeah)

There's a better day coming, I know, I know
(There's a better day coming)
(There's a better day)
(There's a better day coming) I know
(There's a better day coming) Oh
(There's a better day coming) And again, I say rejoice

Chapter 12

My Eyes Have Seen You

When I was a little girl, I always imagined the ocean in person. I heard other people describe it and saw it in pictures, but I couldn't grasp its beauty until the day I saw it with my own eyes. My mom wanted my siblings and me to experience the vast waters, but there were a few obstacles to consider. First, my mom was a single parent at the time, and second, she had four children ranging from four to ten years old. I mean, was she going to take four kids to see the ocean by herself? Yes. That's exactly what she did. After a little begging on our part, mom packed our car, and we were on our way.

My brother and I took turns sitting up front in her Honda Accord. That seat held stiff responsibility, because whoever sat there had to know how to read a map. Thankfully, we were pretty fast learners, so we did our best to help navigate the family. As we neared Myrtle Beach, I kept my eyes glued on the horizon so I wouldn't miss what I had only previously imagined. And peaking between the tall buildings, I finally caught sight of the endless blue waters.

Once parked, we ran out onto the warm sand along the shoreline. Our feet sank into the water as small ripples rolled over our toes. We were thrilled to have made the nine-hour trip. It was then that we each had words of our own to describe what we saw and felt. And in a single moment, our perception of the world widened.

Personal experiences have a way of changing us. Most often, we are never the same after such encounters. On the contrary, it's hard to describe something that we've never seen or witnessed. For example, can you put the taste of food you've never eaten into words? You can attempt to do so, but who will believe your explanation?

Experiencing God is like this. Until we personally meet with Him, all we have are the words of others and our misperceptions.

In John Chapter 4, Samaritans initially believed in Christ based on the words of one woman. This woman drew water at a well that Jesus was sitting by. While there, Jesus asked her to give Him a drink. Startled, the woman told Christ that she was a Samaritan and He was a Jew. How could Jesus ask her for a drink if Jews didn't associate with Samaritans? Jesus explained to her that if she knew who it was asking her for the drink, she would be the one asking Him, and He would give her living water.

This living water intrigued the woman, prompting her to ask Jesus for some so she wouldn't have to return to the well. Before He proceeded, Jesus told her to get her husband. These words are essential because Christ gave the woman an opportunity to confess her sins. First, she tells the Lord that she doesn't have a husband. Then Christ clarifies that she is right though she has had five husbands and the man she is currently with isn't her husband. By the end of the encounter, the woman acknowledges that Jesus is a prophet though she still doesn't see His true identity.

The woman said, "I know that Messiah" (called Christ) "is coming. When he comes, he will explain everything to us."
Then Jesus declared, "I, the one speaking to you--I am he."
—John 4:25-26, NIV

It's obvious the woman had never personally experienced God because she was speaking to Him without realizing it. She didn't consider Christ until after He revealed Himself to her. Once He did, she went back to the town and said to the people:

"Come, see a man who told me everything I ever did. Could this be the Messiah?" They came out of the town and made their way toward him.
—John 4:29-30, NIV

The words of one woman convinced many others to inquire of the Lord. But their faith wasn't certain until they experienced Him themselves.

They said to the woman, "We no longer believe just because of what you said; now we have heard for ourselves, and we know that this man really is the Savior of the world."
—John 4:42, NIV

In other words, these men went from initially believing to making their hope sure. This is the difference between infant and mature faith. If the men never went to Christ themselves, their perception of Him would solely rest on the woman's words. Their infant faith would never be enough to sustain them through the trials of life. But experiencing the Lord personally increased their probability of staying committed to Him. Clinging to the words of others will not support a maturing faith, and neither will our misperceptions.

Job is an example of one who wrestled with words to support his weak position. He somehow endured immense suffering without blaming God, but as we learned earlier, he did say some things that questioned God's actions. However, as he neared the end of his suffering, his discourse with God led to his repentance. Job told the Lord that he previously spoke of things that he didn't understand, things too wonderful for him to know (Job 42:3). In his confession, the Lord opened Job's eyes. And standing in awe of His power, Job responded with these life-changing words:

My ears had heard of you but now my eyes have seen you. Therefore I despise myself and repent in dust and ashes.
—Job 42:5-6, NIV

With remorse, Job acknowledged his misguided thoughts. And for the first time, he saw God for who He truly is. Like Job, we have our thoughts about God, but how many of them are rooted in truth? It's tempting in our suffering to rehash words we've heard others say. Or say things about the Lord that do not represent His character. But God's thoughts are so far above ours that we cannot possibly understand everything His hand permits (Isaiah 55:8). So, at this point in your journey, I pray your eyes have been opened to the wonder of your Creator even if you can't explain His ways.

Jesus says in Luke 11 that our eyes are the lamps of our bodies. When our eyes are bad, our whole bodies are full of darkness. But when they are good, others can even see the light. Knowing this truth, what are we fixing our gaze on? Relying on other people to authenticate God will not improve our vision. We cannot form opinions about a God we do not know or a God that we've never trusted. Personally experiencing Him is how we obtain His light. Because in Him, there is no darkness (1 John 1:5).

So we are lying if we say we have fellowship with God but go on living in spiritual darkness; we are not practicing the truth. But if we are living in the light, as God is in the light, then we have fellowship with each other, and the blood of Jesus, his Son, cleanses us from all sin.

—1 John 1:6-7, NLT

If we are having fellowship with God, we cannot live in darkness because Jesus is the light that has come into the world. People who live in darkness do so because they choose to (John 3:19). Why is that? They do not want their evil desires exposed for everyone to see (John 3:20). But we who live by the truth have the light of Christ. There is a difference between living in spiritual darkness and being in the dark regarding God's plans for our lives. Spiritual darkness occurs when we do not live according to God's Word. But if we have a relationship with Christ, He will give us understanding as we seek Him. This is how believers obtain clarity even in confusing times. We can't always explain God's actions when it comes to the circumstances of our lives, but we can fill ourselves with His light as we fellowship with Him.

Reflecting on our relationships with the Lord, what evidence do we have of His presence? Who is it that we claim He is? Our confession of Christ acknowledges His Spirit within us. Jesus even asked His closest followers who they believed He was.

Jesus and his disciples went on to the villages around Caesarea Philippi. On the way he asked them, "Who do people say I am?"
They replied, "Some say John the Baptist; others say Elijah; and still others, one of the prophets."

—Mark 8:27, NIV

Do you see how the opinions of others can distort the identity of God? According to the nearby communities, Jesus was one of many different people. Some thought He was John the Baptist. Others said He was Elijah or one of the prophets. But Christ was none of those people. So, after asking about the crowd's opinion, Jesus turned and made the question personal:

"But what about you?" he asked. "Who do you say I am?"
Peter answered, "You are the Messiah."
—Mark 8:29, NIV

Well done, Peter! We could have put a gold star by his name if he'd been in Sunday school. Only the Holy Spirit could enable Peter to state the truth (1 Corinthians 12:3). The same question points in our direction. Who do we say Jesus is? Is He our friend on the weekends? Or is He our personal Lord and Savior? We must be able to confess His identity. Our association with Him is not one to escape when trials arrive. If we distance ourselves, then we are back to walking in darkness. John, the apostle, introduces Christ most beautifully:

In the beginning was the Word, and the Word was with God, and the Word was God. He was with God in the beginning.
—John 1:1-2, NIV

Jesus has always existed and has given life to everything He's created. He was present before the Earth appeared, and He'll be present at its destruction (Revelation 22:13).

God created everything through him, and nothing was created except through him. The Word gave life to everything that was created, and his life brought light to everyone. The light shines in the darkness, and the darkness can never extinguish it.
—John 1:3-5, NLT

No matter what falsehoods are spoken against Christ, His light will shine forever. He became flesh and made His dwelling among us. We who believe in Him have seen His glory (John 1:14). We can testify that His life has brought light to the world if we have experienced Him ourselves.

There is no place I'd rather be than in the presence of God. Have you ever spent time with Him and not wanted to leave? We all have busy schedules, but when we have the opportunity to feel the Spirit in a revelational way, it's hard to move past the moment to fulfill the obligations of life. The good news is that He goes with us everywhere we go (Hebrews 13:5). Even when our circumstances change.

When I questioned the Lord about His calling on my life to write the words you are reading, one of my most significant obstacles was making sense of His timing. I argued that my husband's professional baseball experiences were fading each year that passed. Why would someone read about something that was becoming very insignificant to me? I uttered these words when I was attempting to write a memoir; however, I fought to see the effect of our story as time passed.

You also may be in a place where time is blocking your ability to see purpose in your calling. But when the Lord gives you a word, He's already present in the outcome.

Come near me and listen to this: "From the first announcement I have not spoken in secret; at the time it happens, I am there."
—Isaiah 48:16, NIV

God exists in our futures. Right now, He is standing by our side for moments we have yet to experience. And when He reveals something to us regarding our future, His words are not spoken in secret. If God's words were secretive, He would never share them with us. We who obey the Lord are His friends. Servants do not know their master's business, but Jesus calls us friends because He makes known to us what He learns from the Father (John 15:15). We do not have to question the years that pass in between His calling and the fulfillment of His words. If He says it, that settles it.

The Lord's patience will always exceed our faithfulness. I say this because we are not perfect. Consider the amount of faith God says it takes to move a mountain: a mustard seed (Matthew 17:20). If you've ever looked at mustard seeds, you understand how tiny they are. Can you give God that amount of your faith to believe what He's called you to do? Or what He's called you to let go of? Big things happen with a mustard seed of faith, but a harvest erupts when we surrender everything.

"Very truly I tell you, unless a kernel of wheat falls to the ground and dies, it remains only a single seed. But if it dies, it produces many seeds. Anyone who loves their life will lose it, while anyone who hates their life in this world will keep it for eternal life."
—John 12:24-25, NIV

If Christ had not shed His blood on the cross, we would not have the hope of salvation. His willingness to fall to the ground signifies His willingness to go all the way. Jesus didn't partially die for us because none of us would receive redemption if that were the case. No, He went all the way, taking all the sins of the world upon Himself so that we who believe in Him would receive eternal life. Christ's death produced a harvest, unlike anything we can imagine.

The words Jesus spoke above, when He predicted His death, describe the significance of His sacrifice. The same commitment is required of us.

We who believe in Christ must be willing to fall to the ground and die in order to produce a harvest for His kingdom. If we hold onto this life, unwilling to fall, then we will lose the hope of eternal life with Christ. Jesus must be more important to us than anything we could ever gain from the world. And since we are passing through, letting go of this life should be our aim. Does it hurt to lose what we've acquired or what the Lord has allowed us to experience? Certainly. But serving Him means we must follow Him. God the Father will honor those who serve His Son (John 12:26).

When we agree with the Lord to fulfill His will, there will always be friction to halt our commitment. Jesus experienced this before His death when He said that His heart was troubled (John 12:27). He knew what He had to do, but there was the issue of pain and suffering that attached itself to the mission.

"Now my soul is troubled, and what shall I say? 'Father, save me from this hour?' No, it was for this very reason I came to this hour. Father, glorify your name!"

—John 12:27, NIV

Are we supposed to ask God to save us from what He's called us to do so that we won't endure pain or hardship? Jesus says that we are not to do so. Our experiences are to bring the Father glory. And what is produced in return? An eternal harvest.

Whatever was to our profit in this life we must now consider a loss for the sake of Christ (Philippians 3:7). Nothing compares to the surpassing greatness of knowing Christ Jesus our Lord (Philippians 3:8). Paul says that we who are mature should take such a view of things. And if we ever think differently, God will make the truth clear to us. Moving forward, let us live out what we have already attained (Philippians 3:15-16). Contentment helps us put truth into perspective and enables us to press on towards the goal for which God has called us heavenward.

Not that I was ever in need, for I have learned how to be content with whatever I have. I know how to live on almost nothing or with everything. I have learned the secret of living in every situation, whether it is with a full stomach or empty, with plenty or little. For I can do everything through Christ, who gives me strength.

—Philippians 4:11-13, NLT

Philippians 4:13 is often misquoted. God is not saying we can do anything we want. He is telling us, that with Him, we can do anything He's called us to do. Some of us are going to accomplish His will with plenty and others are going to do it with little. And still, some of us will do it experiencing both scenarios. No matter the circumstance, the Lord gives us strength to do what He's called us to complete. He alone is the source of our contentment. When we don't agree with Him, regarding His plans for us, then contentment is not possible. In that space, we will always believe that the grass is greener on the other side of the fence, even though the other side doesn't include the Lord.

For a very long time, Josh looked at the other side of the fence by comparing himself to others. More specifically, Josh's spirit was unable to settle because he wasn't content. He didn't like where he was, and since he couldn't understand it, he wanted something different. Some people work their whole lives to achieve their dreams. They enjoy the fulfillment of these dreams later in life. But Josh achieved his dream early on. So, losing his career in his twenties made starting over unbearable. He couldn't possibly fathom doing anything other than what he'd always known. Over time, his bitterness prevented him from being content. What he failed to realize for many years was contentment comes only from the Lord. We can't be content on our own no matter how many times we adjust our attitudes because feelings change like the shifting wind. We can wake up one day and love our jobs and wake up the next day and hate them.

But when we walk in the light of Christ, and seek His face, gratitude begins to emerge from our hearts. We begin to thank God for what we have rather than fight Him over what we've lost. Opportunities then come our way to minister to others.

When Josh came to a place where he was more thankful than bitter, the Lord provided him with fulfilling opportunities in his new career. Time and time again Josh has ministered to countless teenagers. He has come home excited over what the Lord has allowed him to do. And you know what? Many of these appointments did not involve baseball.

We who seek the Lord lack no good thing (Psalm 34:10).

Regardless of our struggle or loss, if we seek the Lord, we will never lack anything. Life is not characterized by what we've lost, it's defined by what we have. And we have Christ. He alone is enough.

Sing joyfully to the Lord, you righteous; it is fitting for the upright to praise him. Praise the Lord with the harp; make music to him on the ten-stringed lyre. Sing to him a new song; play skillfully, and shout for joy. For the word of the Lord is right and true; he is faithful in all he does.

—Psalm 33:1-4, NIV

It is fitting for us to praise the Lord. What new song can you sing to Him? Maybe you can offer a prayer of thanksgiving, a song of gratitude, or a word of encouragement. If you're like me, you may not be much of a singer. When God made me, He must have said, "Honey, you'll sing to me when you get to heaven. Until then, I need you to write some things down." And you know what? I'm okay with that. I get to enjoy other people using their voices to praise the Lord. The point is, how can we praise He who formed our hearts and considers everything we do? After we've tasted and seen that the Lord is good, we need to tell Him.

But as for me, I will always have hope; I will praise you more and more. My mouth will tell of your righteous deeds, of your saving acts all day long -- though I know not how to relate them all. I will come and proclaim your mighty acts, Sovereign Lord; I will proclaim your righteous deeds, yours alone. Since my youth, God, you have taught me, and to this day I declare your marvelous deeds.

—Psalm 71:14-17, NIV

We do not have to know the measure of God's salvation to tell of His worthiness. Our hope is in Him, and others need to see this hope. Early in life, I saw the hope of Christ in my mom and in others at church. God's light shone in them, and I wanted to know Jesus so that one day I could go to heaven and be with Him forever. I asked Jesus to forgive me of my sins at the age of four. Yes, that's very young. But the Spirit draws people of all ages to the Father. My mom gave me a Precious Moments Bible, and even though I didn't fully understand God's ways, I believed what He said. Child-like faith is believing what God says without having all the answers. Each of us must have this type of faith to inherit eternal life (Matthew 18:3).

Life doesn't truly begin until we acknowledge our need for salvation, asking Christ to forgive us of our sins. Only when we come into a relationship with Him can we begin to live our lives according to His Word. Since my early childhood, God has taught me His ways. He has been with me as I meandered through my teenage years, struggled to find my purpose through my twenties, and questioned Him in my thirties. With Christ comes security. We don't have to know what tomorrow holds before we live today. Our praises to Him should not be subject to our feelings that change because God never changes. We praise the Lord because He is our Savior, and His Word is truth (John 17:17).

But I trust in your unfailing love. I will rejoice because you have rescued me. I will sing to the Lord because he is good to me.

—Psalm 13:5-6, NLT

All praise and glory and honor be to God for rescuing us! Not only does Christ provide salvation, but He protects, mends, restores, and heals. The Lord is good to us, and we have confidence in His redeeming power because He has made the way to Him known (John 14:4). We do not have to walk in darkness or estrange ourselves from Him when we disagree with His plans.

Ask,

Seek,

Knock,

Repeat (Matthew 7:7)

We are asking the Lord questions, we are seeking Him for clarity, and we are knocking on His door to enjoy fellowship. Life with our Creator is a beautiful journey. We are not walking blindfolded through life, scared to take our next step, because the Lord orders all our steps (Proverbs 20:24). He is not our enemy. That role belongs to Satan, and Satan's time is almost up.

The devil isn't all-knowing like God, but he is all-accusing. He accuses us day and night before the throne of God, pointing his finger at our faith (Revelation 12:10). He either accuses us of being unfaithful to God or becoming unfaithful to Him. We saw this in the life of Job. The enemy told God that Job was only faithful to Him because the Lord protected Him. But if God allowed his circumstances to change, then Job would deny Him (Job 1:9-11). We know that didn't happen. Job remained faithful to the Lord because he loved Him more than the world. This is the place we must desire to dwell. Again, our commitment transforms us into overcomers.

Then I heard a loud voice in heaven say: "Now have come the salvation and the power and the kingdom of our God, and the authority of his Messiah. For the accuser of our brothers and sisters, who accuses them before our God day and night, has been hurled down. They triumphed over him by the blood of the Lamb and by the word of their testimony; they did not love their lives so much as to shrink from death. Therefore rejoice, you heavens and you who dwell in them! But woe to the earth and the sea, because the devil has gone down to you! He is filled with fury, because he knows that his time is short."
—Revelation 12:10-12, NIV

Satan's time to steal, kill, and destroy us is almost up, so he's working extra hard in our lives to get us off the path that Christ designed for us. Remember, our struggle is not with each other, and it's not with God; it's with Satan (Ephesians 6:12). Confirming this truth allows us to stay on the narrow path that leads to life. We overcome the enemy by the blood of Christ and the word of our testimonies. Regardless of what we face, unless we follow the Lord, we will not have a testimony to stand on.

Let's turn our eyes upon Jesus, and look fully into His wonderful face, so the things of Earth will grow strangely dim in the light of His glory and grace. May the light of Christ shine brighter in your life than any pain you've carried. To captives, God says, "Come out," and to those living in darkness, He says, "Be free!" (Isaiah 49:9).

God loves you and has equipped you to accomplish His work!

A Prayer for Your Journey:

Lord, thank you for setting me free. You have provided everything I need to journey with you, and life with you is better than anything I could ever experience on my own. Help me stay the course because I've learned that I can overcome the enemy by the blood of Christ and the word of my testimony. Thank you for restoring my faith in you. In Jesus' name, I pray, Amen.

A Hymn to Ponder:

Turn Your Eyes[21]

Song By: Sovereign Grace Music

Turn your eyes upon Jesus
Look full in His wonderful face
And the things of earth will grow strangely dim
In the light of His glory and grace

Turn your eyes to the hillside
Where justice and mercy embraced
There the Son of God gave His life for us
And our measureless debt was erased

Jesus, to You we lift our eyes
Jesus, our glory and our prize
We adore You, behold You, our Savior ever true
Oh Jesus, we turn our eyes to You

Turn your eyes to the morning
And see Christ the lion awake
What a glorious dawn, fear of death is gone
For we carry His life in our veins

Jesus, to You we lift our eyes
Jesus, our glory and our prize
We adore You, behold You, our Savior ever true
Oh Jesus, we turn our eyes to You

Turn your eyes to the heavens
Our King will return for His own
Every knee will bow, every tongue will shout
'All glory to Jesus alone!'

Jesus, to You we lift our eyes

---

[21] "Turn Your Eyes • the Glorious Christ Live." 2019. www.youtube.com. December 10, 2019. https://www.youtube.com/watch?v=F2tKVqZZiI4.

Jesus, our glory and our prize
We adore You, behold You, our Savior ever true
Oh Jesus, we turn our eyes to You

Jesus, to You we lift our eyes
Jesus, our glory and our prize
We adore You, behold You, our Savior ever true
Oh Jesus, we turn our eyes to You
Oh Jesus, we turn our eyes to You

Is Christ Your Personal Lord and Savior?

This book was written for Christians seeking freedom and restoration. But I know not everyone who has picked up this book is a Christian. So, I want to give you the opportunity to make the most important decision of your life.

Becoming a follower of Christ is not difficult. It requires child-like faith. The Lord gives us simple instructions in the book of Acts. *"Believe in the Lord Jesus, and you will be saved."* (Acts 16:31, NIV).

Who do we believe Jesus is? He is the Son of God who came into the world, died on the cross for our sins, and rose from the grave. All who believe in Him will not perish but have eternal life (John 3:16). As the Spirit draws you, take a moment to pray the following prayer:

Jesus, thank you for dying on the cross for my sins. I believe that you are the Son of God and that you are the only way to heaven. Today I repent of the sins I have committed, and I ask that you forgive me so that I can live eternally with you. In Jesus' name, I pray, Amen.

Name:________________________________

Date:_________________________________

Welcome to the family of God! My prayer is for you to dive deeper into God's Word so that you can know Him better!

About Kharis Publishing:

Kharis Publishing, an imprint of Kharis Media LLC, is a leading Christian and inspirational book publisher based in Aurora, Chicago metropolitan area, Illinois. Kharis' dual mission is to give voice to under-represented writers (including women and first-time authors) and equip orphans in developing countries with literacy tools. That is why, for each book sold, the publisher channels some of the proceeds into providing books and computers for orphanages in developing countries so that these kids may learn to read, dream, and grow. For a limited time, Kharis Publishing is accepting unsolicited queries for nonfiction (Christian, self-help, memoirs, business, health and wellness) from qualified leaders, professionals, pastors, and ministers. Learn more at: About Us - Kharis Publishing - Accepting Manuscript

www.ingramcontent.com/pod-product-compliance
Lightning Source LLC
Chambersburg PA
CBHW051425090426
42737CB00014B/2840